School Resilience Planning

A Practical Guide to Emergency Management and Business Continuity Management for Schools

Andrew Fyfe

authorHOUSE®

AuthorHouse™ UK Ltd.
500 Avebury Boulevard
Central Milton Keynes, MK9 2BE
www.authorhouse.co.uk
Phone: 08001974150

© 2010 Andrew Fyfe. All rights reserved.

No part of this book may be reproduced, stored in a retrieval system, or transmitted by any means without the written permission of the author.

First published by AuthorHouse 1/4/2010

ISBN: 978-1-4490-3025-4 (sc)

This book is printed on acid-free paper.

Contents

Glossary	ix
Foreword	1
1. Introduction	3
2. Anticipation	6
2.1 Rationale For School Resilience Planning	6
3. Assessment	8
3.1 Background	8
3.2 Hazards / Threats	8
3.3 Risk Assessment	10
3.4 Health And Safety Policy	12
3.5 Resource Assessment	13
4. Preparation – Overview	15
4.1 Overview Of Preparation Phase	15
4.2 Anatomy Of An Emergency	15
5. Preparation – Planning Strategies	19
5.1 Fire / Explosion At School	19
5.2 Incident During School Activities Off School Premises	20
5.3 Accidental Death Or Injury On School Premises	21
5.4 Violent Intruder Within The School – Incident Ongoing	22
5.5 Violent Intruder Within The School – Incident Over	23

5.6 Multiple Illnesses / Contagious Disease During
School Hours   25

5.7 Criminal Threat Reported In Vicinity Of School   26

5.8 Industrial Hazard In School Vicinity   26

5.9 Accidental Death Or Injury Off School Premises,
Not In School Time   27

5.10 Summary Of Contingency Strategies   27

6. Prevention   29

7. Preparation & Response – The Emergency
Response Plan   32

7.1 Introduction   32

7.2 The School Emergency Response Plan   32

7.3 Emergency Response Plan - Aim & Objectives   33

7.4 Key Locations   34

7.5 Roles & Responsibilities   34

    7.5.1 Emergency Point Of Contact   34

    7.5.2 Emergency Contact For Out Of Hours /
Overseas Trips   35

    7.5.3 Incident Management Team (IMT)   35

    7.5.4 School Community   37

    7.5.5 Local Authority Assistance   38

7.6 Activation Of The Emergency Response Plan   40

7.7 Immediate Response To An Incident On A
School TrIp   40

7.8 Immediate Response To An Incident At The
School   44

    7.8.1 Immediate Actions   44

    7.8.2 Courses Of Action   46

    7.8.3 The Scene   47

    7.8.4 Evacuation   47

7.8.5 Shelter Within The School	48
7.8.6 "Lockdown"	48
7.8.7 Toxic Plume	49
7.8.9 Contagious Illness	50
7.8.10 Bomb Threat	51
7.9 Ongoing Management Of The Incident	52
7.10 Communicating With The School	54
7.11communicating With Parents	57
7.12 Plan Appendices	58
7.12.1 Critical Contact Information	59
7.12.2 IMT Emergency Operations Centre (EOC)	59
7.12.3 IMT Emergency Off-Site Pack	60
7.12.4 Teacher "Grab Bags"	61
7.12.5 Media Packs	62
7.12.6 Log Books	62
8. Response - Strategies For Managing Parents	64
8.1 Parents Of Children Involved But Uninjured	65
8.2 Parents Of The Injured	66
8.3 Bereaved Parents	66
8.4 Parents Of The Remainder Of The School Community	68
8.5 Reception Of Parents At School	68
8.6 Collection Of Children By Parents	69
8.6.1 Control Measures For Collection	70
9. Response - Strategies For Managing The Media	71
10. Response & Recovery - Strategy For School Closure	74
11. Recovery Strategies	77

11.1 Management Of The Physically Injured	78
11.2 Management Of Those Psychologically Injured	78
11.3 Recovery Considerations - Fatalities	80
11.4 Continuation Of Education	81
11.5 Disaster Funds	82
12. Training, Exercising, Maintaining And Review	83
13. Business Continuity Management	85
13.1 BCM Programme	86
13.2 Understanding The Organisation	87
13.2.1 Business Impact Assessment	87
13.2.2 Resource Assessment	89
13.2.3 Risk Review	92
13.3 Determining The BCM Strategy	93
13.4 Developing And Implementing A BCM Response	94
13.5 Exercising, Maintaining And Reviewing BCM Arrangements	96
13.6 Embedding BCM In The Organisation's Culture	96
14. Conclusion	97
Annex A - School Emergency Response Plan Template	100
Annex B - School Business Continuity Management Programme Template	122
Annex C - Sample School Exercises	130
Bibliography	135
About The Author	139

GLOSSARY

BC	Business Continuity
BCM	Business Continuity Management
BCP	Business Continuity Plan
CCTV	Closed-Circuit Television
CRB	Criminal Records Bureau
EOC	Emergency Operations Centre
FLO	Family Liaison Officer
FCO	Foreign and Commonwealth Office
GPS	Global Positioning System
ICP	Incident Control Point
IEM	Integrated Emergency Management
IMT	Incident Management Team
LA	Local Authority
MCA	Mission Critical Activity
MTPD	Maximum Tolerable Period of Disruption
RTO	Recovery Time Objective

FOREWORD

This Practical Guide is the result of several years of work. During my time working as an Emergency Planning Officer, and later Resilience Manager, with Buckinghamshire County Council, it was noticeable that there was a lack of generic guidance available to school resilience planners. Internal guidance documents have been produced both by that Council and numerous others to pull together suitable guidance which has filled the gap, but usually this has been done on an *ad hoc* basis and the level of follow-up has often been limited, through lack of time and resources, to a seminar or several hours of training provided by Emergency Planners. Other sources of guidance include the UK's Teachernet website (www. teachernet.gov.uk) which provides some plan guidance, but which is not extensive. The provision of assistance to non public sector schools can only be imagined.

The current approach has its drawbacks as the guidance given is often quite general and focuses only on the emergency plan content – it does not put the planning phase into an overall context explaining why the plan should be how it is, nor do they explain the full risk assessment process and the rationale for selecting specific response strategies. Furthermore, not all teachers would have been able to attend training and often this would be too short to be truly meaningful.

Although this Practical Guide cannot replace hands-on training, it does at least explain the process in its entirety, providing a cradle to grave approach. The reader, better understanding the context, should therefore be able to understand why a plan includes what it does – this is especially important for independent schools who do not have direct support from the Local Authority. The availability of this guide should also allow Council Emergency Planners and their associated school services to focus on training, rather than spend time creating a guide and then training teachers.

Generally, Business Continuity Management (BCM) has been overlooked compared with emergency response planning. Although related and with similar structures and some processes, BCM is not the same as emergency management. Its focus is the survival of the school 'business', providing guidance to school managers as to its priorities of recovery and providing a mechanism that will ensure the continuation of the critical elements of that business. School emergency management on the other hand focuses on the response to a specific emergency which is threatening the lives or health of its community or property. Most emergency responses will have an element of BCM, but not all threats to the school business will require an emergency response. This Guide attempts to rectify the lack of BCM guidance by providing a possible method, based on the British Standard BS:25999.

In writing this book I would like to thank those who have who have supported me during its preparation. Specifically, thanks are due to my wife Aleksandra, who has suffered many hours of intermittent tapping at the computer with good grace. Also to my father, Alastair Fyfe, and brother-in-law, David Bradbury, (a Governor and assistant head teacher respectively) who read the first drafts for initial feedback. Finally to Arthur Rabjohn, President of the International Association of Emergency Management (IAEM) Europa Council, for his extremely useful comments from a technical aspect, and indeed his views from a seminar in 2004, and Lucy Easthope, my former tutor at the University of Hertfordshire and currently a lecturer at Lancaster University, for her support and comments.

1. INTRODUCTION

The purpose of this book is to provide practical, realistic guidance for teachers and school governors from primary and secondary schools who are involved in School Resilience Planning in the United Kingdom. Resilience Planning combines Emergency Management (EM) - the ability to respond to emergencies that pose, or have the potential to pose, a threat to life or limb to members of the school community and potentially a significant impact to property and the environment - and that of Business Continuity Management (BCM), which ensures that a school can continue its critical activities in the event of a disruption to the school's normal operation. The output of resilience planning is a school emergency response plan and a business continuity plan.

Emergency Management and Business Continuity Management are closely related and share the same response management structures. However, whereas almost all emergency responses will require an element of business continuity to be considered, not all BCM incidents pose a threat to life or limb, and therefore will not require the implementation of a full emergency response. In this book, BCM will be considered both as a stand-alone skill to manage generic disruptions to normal services, for example, a teacher's Union strike, as well as a feature of the response to an emergency.

In the context of this book, an emergency is defined as an incident and its associated consequences. These consequences may be severe and could include the death of, or physical / psychological injury to, members of the school community – both those directly involved in the incident and, for the latter case, those not directly involved. There may also be a significant impact on the school property with cost implications. Any emergency may have a negative impact on the students and therefore its successful management is a prerequisite for moving on to the "new normal" (as opposed to "returning to normality" which presupposes that things could be the same again). The emergency response plan does not replace any fire drills that the school is required to have and test by law, although it will enhance the current school fire drills by considering what happens once the initial evacuation is completed.

To this end, the emergency response plan does not consider the "routine" closures, such as those due to snow or a broken boiler, as an emergency. On the other hand, the consequences of both may be significant in the field of business continuity, as they may see the children away from their education provider for a significant period of time. Such closures may also see a significant impact on the community, with parents having to stay at home to look after their children with wider implications if their jobs are critical to the community infrastructure, such as police, nurses or fire fighters.

Again, for the purposes of this book, 'school community' will be defined as the students, teachers and other school staff. The 'extended school community' refers to the same, plus parents, governors and Local Authority Schools Service. In the context of BCM, 'critical activities' are those activities that the school has determined are essential to be continued (as far as is reasonably practicable) as failure to do so will have a severely damaging impact on the school – in the private sector this might also include the actual survival of the school itself.

The book is aimed primarily at the public sector in the UK, hence references to the Local Authority Schools Service. However, it will not focus on the response by the Local Authority (this should be incorporated into the Authority's Emergency Plan) so the book should be equally practical for both public as well as independent schools. Similarly, as the book considers generic Emergency Management principles, it could be of use to teachers and the management of schools from other countries, not just the UK.

Emergency Management in the context of UK Integrated Emergency Management (IEM), consist of six stages, several of them overlapping - anticipation, assessment, prevention, preparation, response and recovery[1]. Anticipation and assessment are covered in separate chapters. These respectively provide the rationale for resilience planning and the framework around which the plans should be based. Preparation and prevention can occur simultaneously. Prevention is covered in overview as the school will be able to take some measures that may prevent an incident occurring or that might mitigate the impact of an incident if it does occur, but much of the detail of this would fall to experts in fields such as facilities or security management. The preparation and response phases are looked at concurrently as part of the discussion of the plan preparation and implementation. The recovery phase is covered in chapter 11, although again much of the recovery would be guided by specialists, depending on the nature of the incident and its aftermath.

---

1   United Kingdom Cabinet Office (2005). *Emergency Preparedness.* Section 1.42

2. ANTICIPATION

2.1 Rationale for School Resilience Planning

School resilience planning is required for a number of reasons. The purpose of schools is to provide education to children and young people in a safe, learning environment. The potential negative impact - both physically and psychologically - of an emergency on a child or young person cannot be overemphasized and may affect the extended school community and even the wider community.

There are many hazards and threats to schools in modern society – some natural or accidental, and some malicious. School management has a duty of care to its community and in particular the students, who by definition are young and vulnerable. Legislatively, this duty of care is expanded to all those who are legally on the site through the Health & Safety at Work Act (1974). Similarly, there is a duty of care to students under the principle of *'in loco parentis'*.

Outside of the UK, some countries and states make it a formal requirement for schools to have an emergency plan to cover certain hazards. There is no such direct requirement in the UK. However, UK legislation does suggest that not to have a school emergency plan may put the organisation on a tenuous legal footing. The Civil Contingencies Act (2004) requires 'category one responders' (of which the Local Authority is one) to have emergency plans. As the Local Authority is the employer for their schools, the duty might be argued to apply to them, too. The Act also notes that regard should be made towards the 'vulnerable' – a category that includes children. Finally, best practice as directed in the Act, puts forward that all businesses and voluntary organisations should have BCM plans.

Health and Safety legislation requires a school to have a health and safety policy but generally, with the exception of fire safety, guidance on emergency planning or business continuity management is not specified. Fire safety legislation requires a school to have suitable tried and tested procedures for fire evacuation - but how many schools have plans for further evacuation if the school is actually on fire and how many have considered the long term impact of that fire on the return of the school to normal functioning (either due to damage or forensic investigation)?

The health and safety policy might also include reference to other required policies, for example, the schools' off-site trip policy. This book proposes that school resilience planning - specifically the requirement for an emergency response plan and business continuity plan - is included as a requirement in the school's health and safety policy.

3. ASSESSMENT

3.1 Background

Having identified the need for resilience planning, school resilience planners will be required to undertake two assessments, the most important of which is the risk assessment. This identifies for which hazards and threats the planners need to prepare and is the basis of all resilience planning. The school health and safety policy should provide the detailed framework for this undertaking (see section 3.4).

The planner should also undertake a short assessment of current plans and resources available. With regards to plans, this will help avoid duplication and to consolidate previous experience. By assessing resources, the planner will be able to identify a baseline capability against which future resource requirements will be measured.

3.2 Hazards / Threats

To undertake risk assessments, it is first necessary to understand the nature of the risk. School emergencies are caused by hazards or threats affecting the school or school community. Hazards can be considered to be accidental or natural occurrences (e.g. extreme weather, road accident) while threats are those incidents where there is malicious human intent (e.g. terrorism, criminal). Both types will affect the schools in different ways, producing different impacts and consequences. The school emergency response plan should mitigate these impacts and consequences and provide the framework for a managed response to any incident.

Generic hazards and threats should be risk assessed (because they have occurred previously and therefore there is a likelihood that they will occur again).

Possible generic hazards include:

- Fire at the school.
- Explosion (and subsequent fire) at the school.
- Industrial gas (e.g. chlorine) leak / chemical spill / toxic smoke plume affecting the school.
- Accidental death or injury of member of school community on school premises.
- Incident involving a member of school community during school activities off school premises (e.g. day trip / overseas trip).
- Accidental death or injury of member of school community off school premises (not in school time).
- Threat (criminal) reported in the vicinity of the school (but not on school premises).
- Violent intrusion within the school – incident ongoing.
- Violent intrusion within the school - incident over.
- Multiple illnesses or contagious disease amongst the school community, during school hours.
- Bomb threat.

Other hazards or threats can be considered if thought necessary – the risk assessment process should weed out those that do not need to be taken further. For example, in the UK the possibility of a destructive (catastrophic) earthquake is negligible - the risk assessment will place this into a low level risk i.e. one that will not require further planning. Schools in other countries may not have that luxury.

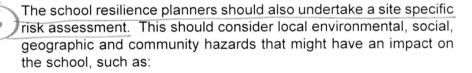

The school resilience planners should also undertake a site specific risk assessment. This should consider local environmental, social, geographic and community hazards that might have an impact on the school, such as:

- Floods (river and flash / surface water flooding)
- Severe weather – storms & gales.
- Local Industrial sites.
- Nearby major transport routes – road, rail or air.
- Community hazards.
- Others (based on geology, geography, meteorology etc of the region).

To help identify possible hazards in the UK, school resilience planners might wish to consult the Community Risk Register prepared by the Local Resilience Forum. Local knowledge and experience will also be of benefit.

School resilience planners should also anticipate future hazards or threats – also known as "horizon-scanning". Local Authority Resilience Teams[2] may also be used to provide input. If a new hazard or threat is identified, the risk assessment process should be utilised as with any other identified hazard.

3.3 Risk Assessment

Risk assessment is used as the basis for emergency response planning as it identifies whether an emergency response plan is required for a specific hazard or threat or not. Resilience planners cannot plan for everything – by adopting this approach, the school resilience planner can identify those hazards for which there is a high likelihood of an occurrence and / or those that will have a particularly high impact. The methodology for the risk assessment needs to be written into the school health and safety policy (see section 3.4).

Essentially, the risk assessment process considers the likelihood and impact of all possible hazards and threats, plotting them onto a risk matrix and giving them an overall risk level. Pre-determined criteria will identify for which level of risk further action is required. Initially, the planners will choose from four generic strategies – to tolerate, terminate, transfer or treat the risk. This decision needs to be taken – or at least confirmed - by the school senior management. For those risks where treat is decided to be the most appropriate strategy, the planner will assess each individual hazard / threat further (chapter 5) in order to prepare his contingency strategies that will be the basis of the school emergency response plan.

In its simplest form each hazard or threat is scored according to a given formula for its assessed likelihood and impact. In the

---

2   A Local Authority in the UK will have teams who are responsible for resilience planning. There are a number of different titles for such teams and their officers, ranging from resilience, emergency planning, emergency management and civil contingency. The term Resilience Teams and Resilience Officers has been used in this guide.

example, the impact has been sub-divided into five levels ranging from insignificant to catastrophic and likelihood has been ranged from negligible to probable. To aid the assessment, impact scores (1 – insignificant, 2 – minor, 3 – moderate, 4 – significant, 5 – catastrophic) can be given definitions while the likelihood scales (1 - negligible, 2 – rare, 3 – unlikely, 4 – possible, 5 – probable) can also be given a numerical basis (such as a one in five years chance of the incident occurring). The hazards and threats are then plotted onto a risk matrix (see table) according to the two scores. The overall risk can then be defined according to the matrix, here from 'low' to "medium", "high" and 'very high'.

I	5 Catastrophic	L	H	VH	VH	VH
M	4 Significant	L	M	H	VH	VH
P	3 Moderate	L	M	M	H	H
A	2 minor	L	M	M	M	M
C	1 Insignificant	L	L	L	L	L
T		1 Negligible	2 Rare	3 Unlikely	4 Possible	5 Probable
	LIKELIHOOD					

Example Risk Matrix

The health and safety policy should identify the threshold level above which the resilience planners need to take further action. This level is called the 'risk appetite' and – bearing in mind the consequences of schools not having appropriate plans – this should be low. Regarding the example risk matrix, the policy might state that 'low' risks can be accepted, but risks graded as 'medium' and above are unacceptable.

Once the hazards and threats requiring further action have been identified, it is necessary to confirm the generic risk strategy to be adopted to mitigate them. Four choices are possible – to tolerate the risk, to terminate the risk by adapting the situation (for example, stopping school trips), to transfer the risk (for example, school trips to be led by another school) or to treat the risk (i.e. preparing an appropriate emergency response plan and enhancing the preventative measures around the school). This choice will need to be confirmed by the school senior management.

As stated earlier, where 'treat' is the chosen generic risk strategy, further assessment of the individual hazards or threats are required (see chapter 5) in order to identify specific response strategies to mitigate the impacts. These specific strategies will then need to be incorporated into the emergency response plan.

The risk assessment should be reviewed annually, but it should be noted that emerging threats or hazards may require the risk assessment to be revised outside these regular reviews.

3.4 Health and Safety Policy

The importance of the school health and safety policy in setting the framework for resilience planning has been noted on several occasions. The policy should include a number of specific details, including:

- Statement identifying who is responsible for resilience planning in the school.
- Statement requiring that the school management team must prepare and maintain an effective emergency response plan.
- Statement that the school must have in place Business Continuity Management (BCM) arrangements including a BCM policy, the need for a BCM Programme and the preparation and maintenance of an effective business continuity plan (chapter 13).
- Statement identifying who is responsible for the completion of the generic risk assessment.
- Statement confirming the methodology to be used for the risk assessment.
- Statement identifying the threshold level (on the risk matrix) for preparing an emergency response or business continuity plan – risk appetite.
- Statement listing the generic hazards and threats that must be considered within a risk assessment.
- Statement confirming for which hazards and threats the school must prepare an emergency plan (based on the risk

assessment).
- Statement confirming for which hazards / threats the school must take into account in a separate school risk assessment.
- Statement identifying a timeframe for reviewing the risk assessment, emergency response plan and Business Continuity Plan.
- Statement confirming the need to be alert to new hazards / threats.

Some Local Authorities may prepare a generic health and safety policy for their schools and may undertake their own risk assessment. If this is the case, each school should always undertake a local risk assessment based on the local hazards or threats around it.

3.5 Resource Assessment

The school resilience planner should carry out an assessment of what plans have already been prepared and what resources are currently available to them for the preparation of the plan and response. Shortcomings may be identified that need to be addressed by the school management or Local Authority. Such an audit might include:

Current policies, plans and other documentation:
- Pre-existing emergency response plan.
- Pre-existing business continuity plan.
- Fire policy.
- School trip policy.
- Health and safety policy.
- School register – location / hard copy / electronic.
- Emergency Next of Kin records.
- Mutual aid agreements with other schools.

Staff:
- How many staff in the school?
- Specialist skills – first aid; media etc.
- Access to educational psychologists.

School facilities:
- Locations – e.g. large halls / gymnasia.
- Potential shelters within the school.

- Entrances / exits.
- Possible assembly areas.
- Possible routes away from the school.
- Car parking / pick-up location.

Communications systems available to school:
- Public address system.
- Radios.
- Telephones and lines out.
- Fax machines available.
- Pagers.
- Bells / alarms / sirens.

Nearby facilities that may be utilised by the school:
- Neighbouring schools.
- Community centres / halls.

Information Technology:
- E-mail / internet / intranet access.
- School Internet site and publishing capability.
- School Intranet site and publishing capability.

Security Systems:
- Fences / gates around perimeter of school
- Entry / egress points to school buildings
- Security Guards
- CCTV systems
- Security measures in place

4. PREPARATION – OVERVIEW

4.1 Overview of Preparation Phase

There are three essential elements to the preparation phase – contingency strategy planning, the preparation of the emergency response plan and the physical preparations required to implement the plan once activated (for example, preparation of media packs, training and exercising).

This chapter initially sets the scene by outlining how an emergency might develop (based on the UK response scenario). Chapter 5 focuses on the planning of strategies based on specific scenarios as identified in the risk assessment. The information from this stage can then be utilised in the preparation of the actual emergency response plan and practical preparations. Chapter 6 considers the concurrent activity of Prevention.

Chapter 7 will look at the preparation of the emergency response plan and in so doing will talk through the response phase of an incident.

4.2 Anatomy of an emergency

To better understand the context of an emergency response plan, it is worth having an understanding of how an emergency develops. This section will outline what may happen at the scene of an incident, whether in the school or off-site, and how the emergency services are likely to respond in the UK. Note that many of the activities will take place concurrently.

An emergency may be caused by a number of different hazards or threats. Initially there will be the scene of the emergency itself. This could be either on or off the school site, or possibly even the entire school site. There may be casualties and fatalities amongst the school community, or students may be involved but not injured.

The emergency services would attend the scene and take control of it, setting up control measures appropriate to the situation, rescuing those who need to be rescued, providing medical aid to the injured and transporting them to hospitals. The uninjured but involved will be required to provide names and contact details for witness statements, and may be taken to hospital for a check-up. The Ambulance Service will coordinate and record the movement of casualties.

Generic roles (not exhaustive) of the emergency services are as follows:

Police:
- Overall coordination of effort through the Incident Control Point (ICP).
- Prevent further criminal activity.
- Establishment of control measures at the scene.
- Record contact details of witnesses.
- Preservation of the scene for forensic investigation.
- Assists HM Coroner in the recovery and identification of the deceased.

Fire and Rescue Service:
- Rescue and recovery of casualties and uninjured.
- Advising on health and safety within the inner cordon.
- Advise on the necessity for further evacuation.

Ambulance Service:
- Treat the casualties.
- Coordinate the distribution of casualties amongst receiving hospitals.
- Transport the casualties to hospitals.
- Record the details of those who have been evacuated and to which hospital they have been taken.

If there are fatalities, they may be left at the scene initially (for forensic investigation) or they may be moved to a temporary body holding area adjacent to the scene. In an incident where there have been a large number of fatalities, the police will not be able to confirm the identity of the deceased until a formal identification process – decided by HM Coroner - has been completed. It should be remembered that some evacuated casualties may subsequently die at, or en route to the hospital, further complicating the identification of the deceased.

The uninjured but involved will be moved to a place of safety where their names can be taken as possible witnesses. Depending on the nature of the incident, these people may be required to go to hospital for a check up. Otherwise, the students should be supervised in a place of safety and where necessary, transport should be organised to return them to the school or their local accommodation.

If the incident is in the school, the school staff will have to manage the incident until the emergency services respond, and then provide support to the emergency services. An individual should be assigned to meet the emergency services on arrival. This individual should be able to escort the emergency services personnel to the scene, provide a verbal briefing regarding the incident and provide them with a floor plan (preferably laminated). This might be kept at the school reception as a matter of course and should be duplicated in the off-site emergency pack (see section 7.12.3).

The school management staff – the Incident Management Team (IMT) - will be required to manage the consequences of the incident, specifically in relation to the immediate impact (physical and psychological) on the extended school community and the ongoing management of the school community and potentially the continuation of school business. Managing the incident may include ordering an evacuation or adopting a shelter strategy for the remainder of the school community.

Parents must be informed and the appropriate arrangements made with (as applicable) bereaved parents, parents of injured children and parents of uninjured children (both directly and indirectly involved in the incident). This may include having special reception arrangements at the school for parents as well as organising special collection procedures for the school. The media are a significant factor in an emergency and will have to be managed carefully. Finally, the school management team will need to manage the short, medium and long-term recovery of the school community.

It should be noted that a school may find itself supporting an emergency response to an external incident - an example of this would be the use of a school as an initial place of safety or rest centre during an evacuation within the local community. The Incident Management Team (IMT) may need to meet to discuss the impacts on the school.

5. PREPARATION – PLANNING STRATEGIES

This chapter takes the results of the risk assessment to the next level. Having identified for which hazard or threat further planning is required, this stage analyses each in turn to define specific strategies to mitigate them. The sections identify a number of considerations for each hazard or threat. These considerations should not be taken as exhaustive but as a guide to identifying strategies that are appropriate for each individual school. The outcome of each individual assessment is a series of strategies that the planner will then need to pull together to create the emergency response plan itself.

During this process, it can be seen that although there are a number of incident types, many of the further considerations are similar and so the generic response will often be the same – the rationale of having a generic school emergency response plan rather than numerous incident specific plans. However, it should be remembered that no two incidents are identical and that the IMT will have to be flexible in the response and adapt to the situation.

5.1 Fire / explosion at school

This hazard is the basis for fire drills already in place at schools and many of the response strategies will already be in place – although it may be worth checking that the assembly area does not infringe upon emergency service access and that there is an alternate assembly area identified in case the primary is inaccessible.

The planners should ensure that in the event that reoccupation is not possible immediately, appropriate measures are available.

Possible consequences, considerations and issues for this type of incident include:

- Evacuate in accordance with fire drill.
- Call emergency services.
- Reporting to fire incident commander.
- Accounting for the school community.
- Control & coordination at assembly area.
- Provide initial parent message.
- Provide initial media message.
- Further evacuation of school community to place of safety.
- Alert & inform Local Authority / School Board.
- Implement medical plans.
- Ongoing media management.
- Ongoing information to parents.
- Invocation of Business Continuity Plan.
- Collection of students by parents.

5.2 Incident during school activities off school premises

This scenario considers the strategies required to respond to an incident involving members of the school community that occurs away from the school – such as a school trip (within the UK or overseas, for any length of time). Such an incident may include the death or injury of a member of the school, a missing child, an intrusion into student accommodation or any other similar incident.

Possible consequences, considerations and issues for this type of incident include:

Scene Management:
- Call emergency services.
- Immediate first aid & prevent further injury.
- Alert & inform IMT.
- Accounting for injured, uninjured & deceased.
- Information updates to IMT.
- Liaise with the emergency services.
- Move students at scene to place of safety / shelter / hospital.
- Onward / return transportation of uninjured students.

Actions of the IMT:
- Establish IMT in the Emergency Operations Centre.
- Communication with emergency services at scene.
- Communicating with Local Authority.
- Communicating with parents of those involved.
- Communicating with the media.
- Implementation of medical plan.
- Coordination of parents to hospital (if appropriate).
- Communicating with school community.
- Communicating with uninvolved parents.
- Organise return / continuation of school trip.

5.3 Accidental death or injury on school premises

This scenario considers the strategies required to respond to an incident involving members of the school community that occurs at the school, but where no foul play is involved.

Possible consequences, considerations and issues for this type of incident include:

Scene Management:
- Call emergency services.
- Immediate first aid & prevent further injury.
- Alert & inform IMT.
- Move students at scene to place of safety.
- Accounting for injured, uninjured & deceased.
- Information updates to IMT.
- Liaise with emergency services on arrival.
- Be prepared to provide witness statements.

Actions of the IMT:
- Establish IMT.
- Ensure Emergency Services escorted to scene; floor plans if required.
- Communication with emergency services at scene (possibly through staff member at scene).
- Communicating with Local Authority.
- Communicating with parents of those involved.
- Communicating with the media.
- Communicating with remainder of school community.

- Communicating with uninvolved parents.
- Consider siblings / friends / classmates / team-mates etc.
- Consider implications of forensic investigations.
- Consider invocation of Business Continuity Plan.

5.4 Violent intruder within the school – incident ongoing

In this scenario, there is an immediate and ongoing threat to the school community. There is at least one scene and the location of the threat is potentially unknown. The scene(s) and probably the entire school will become a crime scene, requiring forensic examination by the police. There may be a number of casualties and / or traumatised members of the school community.

The police will need to locate and isolate any intruder, followed by an efficient and swift evacuation of the school community, so the school response should support this. The initial response is likely to be a lockdown (see section 7.8.6) the subsequent response may call for an evacuation of some or all of the school community, depending on the incident. (Note, in the event of a determined and violent intruder, it would be very difficult to prevent violence, so it is essential that the police are summoned as quickly as possible).

Possible consequences, considerations and issues for this type of incident include:

Immediate response at the scene:
- Call emergency services.
- Immediate first aid & prevent further injury.
- Protect the remainder of the school community – evacuate to safety if possible.
- Shelter, if not possible to evacuate.
- Alert & inform IMT.
- Account for members of the school community at the scene.
- Liaise with the emergency services.

Actions of emergency point of contact:
- Confirm emergency services have been summoned.
- Prepare escort for emergency services.
- Brief the Incident Manager.

Actions of Incident Manager:
- Protect the remainder of the school community:
    - o Evacuate to place of safety where possible.
    - o Lockdown where not possible to evacuate.
- Establish IMT.

IMT response:
- Communicating with the local authority.
- Communicating with the emergency services.
- Manage the developing incident.
- Implement medical plans.
- Alert & inform the Local Authority / School Board.
- Communicating with the school community.
- Communicating with parents.
- Communicating with the media.
- Invocation of Business Continuity Plan.

Actions of school community if instructed to lockdown:
- o Accounting for school community who are sheltering.
- o Ongoing communication with school community within school.
- o Liaison with police regarding those in lockdown.
- o Prepare to evacuate when possible.

Actions of school community if instructed to evacuate:
- First aid where required.
- Evacuate from assembly area to place of safety as quickly as possible.
- Establish IMT at place of safety.
- Accounting for school community at place of safety.
- Liaison with emergency services.
- Liaison with local authority.
- Collection of school community from place of safety.

5.5 Violent intruder within the school – incident over

In this scenario, the threat to the school community is over however there may be multiple incidents and scenes. There may be a number of casualties and traumatised members of the school community. The scene(s) and probably the entire school will become a crime scene, requiring forensic examination by the police. This will impact the school's ability to respond to normal functioning.

Possible consequences, considerations and issues for this type of incident include:

Immediate response at scene(s):
- Call emergency services.
- Immediate first aid & prevent further injury.
- Protect the remainder of the school community – move away from scene(s) to safe location.
- Treat for shock.
- Make available for witness statements.
- Communication between scene and IMT.
- Accounting for injured, uninjured & deceased.
- Escort emergency services to scene(s).
- Treat as crime scene.

Actions of emergency point of contact
- Confirm emergency services have been summoned.
- Prepare escort for emergency services.
- Brief the Incident Manager.

Actions of Incident Manager
- Protect the remainder of the school community – lockdown.
- Establish IMT.

IMT response
- Communicating with the emergency services.
- Manage the developing incident.
- Communicating with the school community.
- Communicating with the local authority.
- Implement medical plans.
- Communicating with parents.
- Communicating with the media.
- Alert & inform the Local Authority / School Board.
- Invocation of Business Continuity Plan.

Actions of those uninvolved and / or the remainder of the school community:
- Secure access / egress to school.
- Accounting for remainder of school community.
- Ongoing communication with school community within school.
- Prepare to evacuate if required.

5.6 Multiple illnesses / contagious disease during school hours

This scenario presupposes a single case of a suspected contagious disease or the sudden onset of the same symptoms of illness in a number of students in a short period of time. If the emergency services cannot identify the illness / cause of the illness, they may treat the casualties as contaminated, requiring mass decontamination. In the UK, the lead will be taken by the Primary Care Trust and the Health Protection Agency.

Possible consequences, considerations and issues for this type of incident include:

Scene Management:
- Immediate first aid (if appropriate).
- Call emergency services.
- Isolate the group(s).
- Segregate symptomatic from non-symptomatic.
- Segregate those non-symptomatic who have been in close proximity to the ill, from those who were not within close proximity.
- Alert & inform the IMT.
- Account for all students.

Actions of the IMT:
- Establish IMT.
- Escort ambulance service to the scene.
- Communicating with the emergency services.
- Communicating with the Local Authority / School Board.
- Communicating with parents.
- Communicating with Public Health doctors.
- Communicating with remainder of school community.
- Communicating with the media.
- Potential lock-down / quarantine of school until clarification of situation.
- Collection of children only on agreement of emergency services.
- Be prepared for possible mass decontamination.
- Invocation of Business Continuity Plan.

Actions of the remainder of the school community:
- Accounting for remainder of school community.
- Lockdown of school community until situation clarified.
- Ongoing communication with school community within school
- Informing parents.

5.7 Criminal threat reported in vicinity of school

This scenario considers the threat of criminal activity outside the school perimeter but close enough to possibly have an impact on school activity – possibly at the beginning or end of the school day. There may be a need to delay the start of the school day or the collection of children.

Possible consequences, considerations and issues for this type of incident include:

Actions of the IMT:
- IMT establishment.
- Secure the school.
- Ensure access / egress to school prevented.
- Informing school community of lockdown.
- Communicating with the emergency services.
- Communicating with the Local Authority / School Board.
- Communicating with parents.
- Communication with school community.
- Managing the collection of children.

5.8 Industrial hazard in school vicinity

This scenario considers the hazard of a plume of potentially toxic smoke or fumes caused by a fire outside the school, an accident in an industrial process or road transport accident. Unless told to evacuate by the fire and rescue service or where there is a specific fire hazard to the school, the usual advice given is "Go in, Stay in, Tune in" – the process of sheltering and tuning in to the local radio station which will be expected to provide further information.

Possible consequences, considerations and issues for this type of incident include:

Actions of the IMT:
- Alerting the school community – lockdown.
- Establish IMT.
- Communicating with the emergency services.
- Communicating with the school community on further actions.
- Move school community to designated safe haven.
- Accounting for school community.
- Communicating with parents.
- Communicating with the media.
- Communicating with Local Authority.
- Provision of 'all clear' message.
- Actions on 'all clear'.
- Invocation of Business Continuity Plan.

5.9 Accidental death or injury off school premises, not in school time

This scenario considers the accidental death of a member of the school community on activities that technically have nothing to do with the school. However, as the child or staff member is a member of the school community the Incident Management Team may well consider it necessary to meet and consider the possible implications of the incident.

Possible consequences, considerations and issues for this type of incident include:

Actions of the IMT:
- IMT establishment.
- Communication with emergency services at scene.
- Communicating with Local Authority.
- Communication with bereaved / parents of injured.
- Communication with remaining parents.
- Liaison with hospital(s).
- Liaison with local authority.
- Informing school community.
- Consider siblings / friends / classmates / team-mates etc.

5.10 Summary of Contingency Strategies

As noted, the list of hazards / threats mentioned in this chapter should not be considered as exhaustive, nor should the considerations provided. However, they provide a start point for resilience planners.

The result of this assessment is a number of strategies that can be collated and formed into a plan. Some strategies will need an element of preparation prior to an incident occurring. This could include identifying locations, ensuring the communications plan is effective, preparing equipment and confirming contact information. Other strategies will be directly written into the emergency response plan as part of the direct response.

Further mitigation measures may also have been identified that might help prevent an incident occurring – or indeed, prevent an incident becoming a crisis. Such measures fall under the heading of 'Prevention' and will be discussed in the next chapter.

It is worth noting that although there are a number of hazards / threats, the impacts of these, and consequently the strategies required to mitigate them, are fewer and can be quite readily condensed into a generic emergency response plan.

6. PREVENTION

The prevention phase takes place concurrently with the preparation phase. By assessing the various hazards and threats, a planner will have identified a number of preventative measures that could be taken to either prevent an incident occurring or to mitigate the impact of an incident should one occur. However, it should be noted that it may not always be possible to prevent a determined threat to a school or prevent an accident – hence the importance of having an emergency response plan to manage an incident when it occurs.

Examples of some preventative measures that might be employed to mitigate specific hazards or threats would include the following:

Fire or explosion:
- Fire alarms.
- Sprinklers.
- Fire doors.

Incident on school activity:
- Security briefing to students.
- Procedure for reporting suspicious activities.

Accident on school premises:
- Health and Safety measures – facilities and procedural.

Intruder onto school premises / threat in the vicinity of the school:
- Security measures – fences, gates, CCTV, security guards
- Security briefing to school community to be observant etc
- Procedure for reporting suspicions
- Facilities – numbers of entry / exit

- New builds – design in security features; emergency egress routes.

Illness on school premises:
- Maintain excellent hygiene regime
- Hygiene awareness instruction for children

Smoke plume / toxic chemical cloud:
- Identified shelter locations
- New build – design in shelter locations

Generic hazards or threats:
- New build – design in control rooms, communications systems, emergency egress

Not all these measures will be actionable by the resilience planner – indeed a business case may need to be made to the school management team in order to get funds for a project.

A simple preventative measure that can be undertaken at minimum cost is ensuring awareness amongst the school community and providing them with an appropriate means of reporting suspicious activities. Previous incidents show that warnings are sometimes given to other students (although not always with sufficient time to act) or suspicions aroused. A reporting mechanism should be provided for the school – it may simply be telephoning the emergency services emergency number if the threat is immediate, or reporting suspicions or concerns to a designated member of staff if not.

Awareness should not simply be limited to reporting suspicious activities. General security awareness should be merged with awareness of hygiene and fire safety. Prior to trips or specific activities, children should be made aware of hazards, how to avoid them and what to do if they happen.

Security measures are an effective deterrent to some criminals. By limiting access and egress points into a school, the management is channelling entry through locations that can be supervised. This can be enhanced by appropriate obstacles (such as fences) in open areas such as playing fields. CCTV has its use, as the mere presence of cameras may deter less determined criminals or those that don't want to risk being caught. However, to be truly preventative it would require a security guard to observe the display and then be able to act on the observations. Having CCTV also has its investigative benefits.

It is not always possible to decide on the level of security required based on the location and environment in which the school is situated – urban schools may seem more likely to need stronger security measures, but rural schools may also need them. Horrific incidents can occur in places that might otherwise be considered relatively safe – for example, at Dunblane primary school in 1996. However, as a general rule, the location and environment should be taken into consideration and appropriate measures taken – balanced against the need for the school to remain a place of education and not a fortress.

Some preventative benefits may derive from the preparation measures that should be being undertaken. For example, first aid training may be provided to prepare staff – and hopefully older children – in the event of an emergency. By knowing the basics of first aid, those individuals could prevent an incident becoming a crisis.

To summarise, the prevention phase occurs concurrently to the preparation phase. It is very much based on the specific situation of the school and its environment, of the resources and funds available to the planners and school management. However, having extensive preventative measures will not guarantee that an incident will not occur – a school emergency response plan remains essential.

7. PREPARATION & RESPONSE – THE EMERGENCY RESPONSE PLAN

7.1 Introduction

As with the prevention phase, there are a number of activities that can be undertaken to ensure that the school is best prepared to respond to an emergency. Essentially however, preparation can be assured by preparing an effective emergency response plan and undertaking all associated activities (e.g. training, exercising, reviewing and maintenance). To this end, the chapter will look at the preparation of the school emergency response plan as the preparation phase. To give it context, the plan will be described concurrently with a discussion of the response phase.

7.2 The School Emergency Response Plan

The emergency response plan provides the framework for the school to respond to any number of emergencies that pose a real or potential threat to the lives of its school community. It should be a stand-alone document - simple, logical and functional. In essence, it should state who does what, when, where, how, with what and how it all works together, yet remain flexible enough to adapt to a number of different situations. All staff must be trained in the emergency response plan and training should be validated through exercises and post-exercise review. The plan should be maintained and reviewed at regular intervals (see chapter 12).

Prior to any plan being prepared, the head teacher will need to identify an individual who will be responsible for the preparation of the emergency plan, its upkeep and its training and exercising regime. Governors should be given the task of auditing the plans. Where relevant to parents, elements of the emergency response plan should be made available in advance.

The emergency response plan is made up of a number of standard features – a template plan is included in Annex A. The basic features of the plan will be discussed in detail below, but essentially they include the following:

- Aim and Objectives of the Plan
- Key locations.
- Generic Roles and Responsibilities.
- Aim of the emergency response.
- Plan activation triggers
- Immediate Actions (first 30 minutes or so).
- Ongoing actions (after the first 30 minutes).
- Logistics.
- Appendices, as appropriate (maps, floor plans etc).
- Contact information.
- Training, exercising, review and maintenance.

7.3 Emergency Response Plan - Aim & Objectives

The purpose of the emergency response plan is to provide a framework for the school's response to an emergency in order to save life and prevent further injury to the school community in the event of a potentially life-threatening emergency.

The objectives of the plan might include:

- To identify the aims and objectives of the plan.
- To describe the locality in general, especially with regards to key locations.
- To describe the school geography in detail, especially with regards to key locations.
- To identify key responders (and deputies) including the Incident Management Team and their generic roles.
- To identify potential triggers for plan activation.
- To describe the activation process.
- To describe the scene management.
- To identify possible hazards and identify appropriate strategies for managing the response.
- To identify the Immediate Actions of the responders and school community.
- To identify how the Incident Management Team will communicate

with the extended school community.
- To identify strategies and tasks for managing the response to various specific hazards.
- To identify strategies and tasks for managing parents.
- To identify strategies and tasks for managing the media.
- To describe control and coordination arrangements.
- To identify critical contact information required in the response.
- To identify a training and exercising schedule.
- To identify a plan audit and review process.

7.4 Key Locations

Several locations and key routes in and near the school should be identified in the plan. These include:

- Primary and secondary Emergency Operations Centre (EOC).
- Primary access and egress into the school.
- Secondary access and egress into the school.
- Assembly area and routes in.
- Alternate assembly area and routes in.
- Sheltering locations within school.
- Designated shelters for outside areas.
- Place of safety (on school site).
- Alternate place of safety (off school site) e.g. "buddy school".
- Route to alternate place of safety.
- Primary reception point for parents.
- Alternate reception point for parents.
- Reception point for parents at place of safety.
- "Quiet room" for the Recovery.

7.5 Roles & Responsibilities

The school emergency plan will need to identify a number of appointments, whose roles are described in the following sections.

7.5.1 Emergency point of contact

An emergency point of contact should be established for the school during normal working hours. Ideally this should be an appointment in a permanently staffed position, such as school secretary, reception or administration position. This point of contact must be available at all times during school hours. Note that although the head teacher is likely to be the Incident Manager, it is not necessarily appropriate to have him / her as the emergency point of contact (he / she may be teaching or just unavailable).

The emergency point of contact should be provided with a copy of the emergency plan and a checklist of actions that will prompt the caller to provide all the required information.

Ideally, the emergency point of contact should be provided with two phones – one for receiving emergency calls and one for communicating out, for example, with the scene or the Incident Manager.

A possible summarised checklist for the emergency point of contact would be:

- Receive call from incident scene.
- Check information against prepared template.
- Call the emergency services / confirm they have been summoned.
- Alert and inform the Incident Manager.
- Alert IMT members and summon to chosen IMT location.
- Inform the Local Authority emergency contact.

7.5.2 Emergency Contact for out of hours / overseas trips

For school trips or activities, standard arrangements should identify an administrative contact within the school to deal with routine issues. For emergencies or serious incidents occurring outside normal working hours, schools should also identify a 24 / 7 emergency point of contact for use by staff members (or students).

For state schools, this may be the Authority's duty Resilience Team contact – which provides a tried and tested procedure that also automatically ensures that the Local Authority is involved from the start. The process for using this contact should be confirmed in school trip procedures – the caller should be required to leave name, school, full contact details (including country code), and should expect to receive a call back quickly.

7.5.3 Incident Management Team (IMT)

The Incident Management Team (IMT) manages the school response to an emergency and coordinates it with other responders, such as the emergency services, local authorities, hospitals etc. A possible

IMT composition, with suggested roles, is shown below:

Incident Manager:
- Leads the response - usually head teacher.
- Takes initial critical decisions.
- Must have the authority to make unilateral decisions if required.
- Maintain a tactical overview of the response.
- Access to student emergency contact detail.
- Available for press conferences, but not the media lead.

Deputy Incident Manager:
- Deputises for the head teacher in absence.
- Coordinates with teachers in the school.
- Responsible for the remainder of the school and BCM.
- Access to student emergency contact details.

Parent Liaison Officer:
- Responsible for coordination of information to parents.
- Coordinates information requests from parents.
- Acts as a point of contact for parents.
- May require a team to support telephones.

Media Liaison Officer:
- Responsible for the preparation of media information packs.
- Point of contact for the Media during the response.
- Provide constant flow of information to the Media.
- Liaise with Local Authority Communications Officer(s) Officer(s) / Police Press Relations Officers.

Logistics coordinator:
- Coordinates logistic / facilities / security related tasks.
- Usually Facilities Manager.

Administration:
- Maintain a log – both for events and decisions.
- Answering telephone calls.
- "Runner" for passing messages.

Representative of Governing Body:
- Often Head Governor.

- Provide the strategic overview of the response from the school perspective.
- Provide a "talking head" (spokesperson) for the Media.

Members of Local Authority:
- For example, education officer, communications (Media) officer, educational psychologist. Deployed on request in accordance with Local Authority generic emergency plan.
- Tasked to support the school's response and to provide coordination between the school and the Local Authority.
- As employer, provides strategic guidance to IMT.

It is appreciated that schools differ widely in staff numbers and the resources available to them, and that in some instances it will be necessary to double up roles.

The head teacher has a large degree of autonomy with regards to managing the incident and would normally be the Incident Manager. The relationship of the head teacher of a state school and the local authority (as employer) should be agreed in advance and written into the local authority's school emergency response procedures.

During an incident, when resources may be scarce, school resilience planners should consider the possibility of requesting immediate assistance from the local authority and / or mutual aid from a neighbouring, unaffected school (on the understanding that this mutual aid agreement is reciprocal). The support that can be provided by the local authority is identified in section 7.5.5.

All allocated appointees should have a trained deputy in case of sickness / absence. Some specific to role training may be required – for example, media training.

7.5.4 School Community

During an incident, the school community can be divided into several categories – those who are at the scene and those who are not (note the scene may or may not be at the school). Those at the scene may also be sub-divided into a number of groups – fatalities, casualties and the uninjured.

Those students and staff at the scene will need to carry out a number of tasks – not least to summon the emergency services and provide first aid, if known.

Those not at the scene may be indirectly or directly threatened by the hazard, in which case they will have to be alerted and carry out appropriate actions. If not, then the Incident Manager will have to consider how much information is appropriate and then issue that information. If the school community knows of the incident, they will need to be kept informed of the developing situation.

All members of the school community – and especially all staff members – should know what to do if an incident occurs. Staff should receive training and practice these drills in exercises.

7.5.5 Local Authority assistance

For state schools, the Local Authority is the employer and therefore has a duty to look after their school population. It possesses a number of useful resources that could assist the school in its response. The IMT should ensure that the local authority is kept informed of the situation as it develops.

Independent schools do not fall into that category, but as a member of the community with a large number of children amongst its population, there would be a requirement for the Local Authority to support the emergency services in their response to such a school, bearing in mind their duties under the Civil Contingencies Act (2004). This does not take away the requirement for all schools to have a robust emergency response plan and business continuity plan of their own.

For state schools, the Local Authority should be alerted to an incident by the school emergency point of contact regardless of whether their response is required or not. The Local Authority's emergency contact details should be written into the school emergency response plan and might be the duty Resilience Officer or a nominated appointment within the Schools Service. Either way, the Local Authority should have a plan in place to pull together a team to support the school on request from the Incident Manager. This team may consist of a number of Services with various roles. Services from the Local Authority that may be able to assist include (note that Service titles / designations may differ between Authorities):

Schools Service / Local Education Authority:
- Manages the response by the local authority through an operational response team.
- Can deploy officers to the school or scene to assist the school response.
- Provides practical or administrative support to the affected school, for example, contacting parents.

Resilience Team / Emergency Management:
- Usually the initial point of contact for emergencies.
- Help coordinate the local authority response.
- Liaison with the emergency services.
- Able to provide an Emergency Operations Centre (EOC) for the Schools Service.
- Can coordinate the establishment of a 'help line' facility (staffed by schools service).
- Subject matter expertise in emergency management and business continuity management.

Media / Communications Officers:
- Professional communications officers available to assist the school if required.
- Liaison with the Police Press Relations Officer.
- Will have contacts with the local and national media.
- Can help with public information message to parents.

Passenger Transportation:
- Available to provide transportation to / from scene as required.

Children's Social Care:
- Will assist in the recovery, coordinating with educational psychologists as required.

Educational Psychologists
- Available to assess the potential risk to the school community and advise on appropriate methods of managing the psychological impact.

Adult Social Care
- Provide support if required to adults in the extended school community – e.g. staff, parents.

Legal
- Will assess legal implications and advise.

Finance:
- Will assess financial implications and advise.
- May be able to advise on emergency payment requirements.

7.6 Activation of the Emergency Response Plan

The emergency response plan activation procedure needs to state specifically the circumstances that will require the plan to be activated, who activates it, how the relevant parts of the school community will be informed (bearing in mind that not all incidents requires a school response) and what the anticipated response should be.

The response to incidents occurring away from the school premises will entail the swift assembly of the IMT, but the remainder of the school community will not be immediately affected.

For an incident occurring on the school site, the response may vary, depending on the type of incident and the appropriate contingency strategy identified in the preparation phase. Two possible options are likely – evacuate or shelter. These will be discussed later (see section 7.8.4 onwards).

The IMT must have a method of alerting the school community in the event of an incident on site that threatens their safety. This alert should provide initial direction to the school community's response. Alerting and informing can be achieved simultaneously by associating a specific alarm with a set procedure – for example, the fire alarm not only alerts the school community to fire, but also informs the school community to evacuate.

7.7 Immediate Response to an Incident on a School Trip

This section considers the response to an emergency that takes place on a school trip, up to the point where the IMT takes on the incident management role, at which point section 7.9 continues.

School trips or activities outside school premises should be covered by a separate school policy requiring specific risk assessments. In preparation, appropriate numbers of staff should be assigned to the trip / activity, depending on the age and numbers of students. A single member of staff should be designated with the responsibility as trip / activity leader and a deputy leader nominated. Members of staff involved in trips / activities should have as a minimum:

- A working mobile phone with charger.
- An understanding of the emergency contact procedure and know the emergency point of contact telephone number for the school and Local Authority.
- A full and accurate register of the children and staff involved in the trip – this will need to be duplicated and a second copy kept available to the IMT.
- A copy of the emergency plan / extracts of relevant elements (checklists etc).
- Suitable first aid training (ideally).
- Other items as detailed in the school's trips policy.

Prior to departure, and at appropriate times during the trip / activity, the students should be given a health and safety brief appropriate to their age and circumstances.

In the event of an incident, the overarching aim is to save life and protect the lives of those others involved. At the incident scene, the member of staff will be required to undertake the following activities (note that several may occur concurrently):

- Save life, if possible.
- Summon the appropriate emergency service(s).
- Protect the lives of remaining students – possibly by moving them to a place of safety.
- Alert the IMT through the emergency point of contact.
- Account for all school community personnel on the trip / activity.
- Provide appropriate information for the IMT.
- Brief the emergency services on numbers of children / details of school.
- If any members of the school community have been taken to hospital, note which students and which hospital (liaise with the Ambulance service representative at the scene).
- Ensure communications available to continue to report to the IMT.

- Manage the incident as best as possible.

The emergency services will need to know the following from the trip / activity leader:

- Which of the emergency services are required?
- Location.
- Group details – include numbers of children and adults.
- What has happened and when.
- What is now happening?
- Is there a continued threat?
- Your contact details.

It is worth noting that using the '112' emergency number from a mobile phone, where the mobile network coverage allows, will ensure that the position of the phone can be identified by Global Positioning System (GPS), aiding the emergency response.

The trip / activity leader will need to alert and inform the school of the incident through the emergency procedures, providing the relevant information to the school emergency point of contact for the IMT (or if out of hours / calling from overseas, this information will go through the Local Authority's 24 / 7 contact number). The following should be provided:

- Own identity and group details.
- Confirm contact details.
- Confirm that the emergency services have been summoned and whether they are on scene.
- What has happened?
- Where did it happen?
- When did it happen?
- Who is involved from the school community and what is their condition?
- Has everyone been accounted for? Where is everyone?
- What is now happening?
- Have any of the school community been taken to hospital? Which hospital?
- Are there any specific requirements from the scene?
- Any other information that the trip / activity leader believes appropriate.

It is unlikely that all information will be available immediately. It is best to provide some information sooner, than all the requested information too late.

Where possible, students should be prevented from making phone calls to anyone except the emergency services, while a semblance of control is established over the situation. This will help to ensure that the school continues to control the release of information.

Where the students are more mature they may be able to actively assist by moving themselves to a designated place of safety, but they should not be put in any further danger doing so.

At the school, the emergency point of contact will inform the Incident Manager or deputy of the details. If utilising the out-of-hours emergency number, the Incident Manager would be informed by the Local Authority contact and will then contact the staff member at the scene directly.

The immediate response by the Incident Manager should include:

- Carry out a rapid impact assessment.
- Convene the IMT in the primary EOC / inform the IMT members if not in working hours.
- Alert the Local Authority Schools Service / Resilience Team according to agreed procedures.
- Re-establish contact with the trip leader for the latest information and to confirm the emergency services are involved.
- Assess the situation and be prepared to take further action, including informing parents / media.

Maintaining communication with the scene is critical. Whilst the staff member who called in the incident is there, she / he can be utilised. However, if this is not possible, the Local Authority Resilience Team may be able to assist by deploying liaison officers to the scene (although this may take some time) or by using their contacts with the emergency services to gather more information. Apart from getting as much information for the IMT, the liaison officer's role would be to provide the emergency services with as much information as possible about those involved in the incident. If overseas, assistance will be required from the tour operator – if one is being used – and the

Foreign and Commonwealth Office (FCO).

7.8 Immediate Response to an Incident at the School

This section considers the immediate incident management response to an emergency occurring on the school premises or threatening the school premises.

An incident within a school may develop in a number of ways, depending on the nature of the hazard or threat and the numerical and physical size of the school. Several strategies may need to be utilised to manage the incident – these are likely to take place concurrently. It should be noted that the IMT and the entire school may be directly involved in the incident, making management of the emergency significantly more complex.

The fact that the school is actively involved in the incident adds to the immediacy of the situation and the need for the effective passage of information and swift decision-making. In such circumstances, the requirement to have a simple plan with alternate locations, deputies and good communications, supported by training and exercising, is critical.

7.8.1 Immediate Actions

The immediate actions of staff involved in, or witnessing, an incident are similar to that of those on a school trip:

- Save life, if possible.
- Summon the appropriate emergency service(s).
- Protect the lives of remaining students – possibly by moving them to a place of safety.
- Alert and brief the IMT through the emergency point of contact.
- Continue to liaise with the IMT as required.
- Brief the emergency services on numbers of children / details of school.
- If any members of the school community have been taken to hospital, note which students and which hospital.
- Manage the incident as best as possible.
- Maintain a log of activities.

Needless to say, if the incident was a fire, then the initial response would be to follow the school's fire procedures and to evacuate to the assembly area.

For other incidents, the emergency point of contact should be alerted. Again, as much information as is available should be provided as quickly as possible - further information can be provided later. The information that will be required should be prepared in a checklist held by all staff and includes:

- Name and location.
- Confirm contact details.
- Confirm that the emergency services have been summoned and whether they are on scene.
- What has happened?
- Where did it happen?
- When did it happen?
- Who is involved from the school community and what is their condition?
- Has everyone been accounted for? Where is everyone?
- What is now happening?
- Have any of the school community been taken to hospital? Which hospital?
- Are there any specific requirements from the scene?
- Any other information that the trip / activity leader believes appropriate.

The emergency point of contact would then alert the Incident Manager. The Incident Manager should ensure that the following actions are taken:

- Identify who is to meet the emergency services, where they will be met and ensure they are escorted to the scene.
- Ensure swift access to the scene.
- Identify who will liaise with the Emergency Services and from where.
- Ensure the emergency services are provided with all information through a single source in order to prevent duplication / confusion.
- Ensure the remainder of the IMT are being alerted.
- Conduct an initial impact assessment.

The Incident Manager should make a rapid impact assessment of the situation in order to decide on the most suitable course of action that will protect the school community at the scene and the remainder of the school who may be indirectly threatened by the hazard. This decision will probably need to be made immediately, without recourse to the full IMT.

Factors to consider in this impact assessment include:

- Confirm the aim - to save life and prevent further injury.
- What is the hazard?
- Where is the hazard?
- Where is the "scene"?
- Where are the school community? Consider those at the scene and the remainder of the school community.
- What are the possible consequences of the hazard to the school community?
- What is the future threat to the school community and how can this be mitigated?

7.8.2 Courses of Action

Following the impact assessment, the Incident Manager will have to make several decisions, including:

- What advice to give to those at the scene.
- How best to protect the remainder of the school community:
  - o Evacuate.
  - o Shelter – lock-down / shelter downwind / quarantine.
- Whether there is a need to alert the remainder of the school and if so, how best could this be done and what message should be provided.
- Where to convene the IMT – primary or secondary EOC.
- Whether to authorise the release of the prepared emergency message to parents immediately.
- Ensure that the Local Authority is informed of the situation.

A critical decision relates to the protection of the school community where there is an ongoing or potential threat. There are essentially two generic options open – to evacuate or shelter. These are discussed further below. Where there is no threat, the IMT will need to decide at what point to inform the school community of the incident and how much information should be provided.

In some circumstances (such as an ongoing violent intrusion) and depending on a number of factors (such as the size of the school, the location of the incident and the intentions of the attacker) the most suitable course of action may be a mixture of evacuation and shelter – a very difficult situation to control and potentially an ethically difficult decision to make. In such circumstances, the best option has to be what is best for the *majority* of the school community, rather than the entire school community. There will have to be some reliance on the personal initiative of staff and even students.

7.8.3 The Scene

Guidance to those at the scene itself will be dynamic as the situation may be changing rapidly. The over-riding aim of the response – to save life and prevent further injury – will be the guiding principle and staff will have to use their initiative to adapt to the situation.

Those at the scene should ensure they move to a safe location immediately. As soon as the emergency services arrive, they will take control of the scene. The staff member will then be required to liaise with the emergency services and provide information to the IMT until replaced.

Where a staff member at the scene is injured, she / he will be evacuated by the emergency services and the IMT will need to establish further liaison with the scene by sending another staff member to the emergency services' control point.

7.8.4 Evacuation

A full evacuation of the school will be required when the best course of action is for the majority of the school community to actively remove themselves from an apparent or physical danger within the school.

The school fire procedures will have identified an assembly area to which students and staff should move. The emergency response plan should identify an alternate assembly area that could be utilised in the event of incidents where the primary assembly area is inaccessible.

Both assembly areas should be easily accessible from the school and should provide an egress route away from the school without having to re-enter the school. The assembly areas should be at a safe enough distance not to be affected by what is occurring in the school and should not cause an obstruction to the emergency services. Standard security measures (for example locked gates and doors) that are designed to protect the school from intrusion should not be allowed to prevent access to the school or egress to the assembly areas in the event of an emergency – spare keys or the lock combinations should be available.

It may be necessary to evacuate beyond the assembly area. The school resilience planner should identify one or more locations or 'places of safety' which are accessible from the assembly area (and alternate assembly area) for onward evacuation. Such 'places of safety' could include other schools, local community centres, halls, sports centres or libraries. It may be appropriate to arrange a reciprocal agreement with another school in the vicinity, a 'buddy school', by which if there was an evacuation from one, the other would provide a place of safety and vice versa. Head teachers of "buddy schools" and proprietors of institutions / hall managers should be consulted in advance.

In some situations, a partial evacuation may be appropriate for a large school, in which case communicating a clear message to those involved in the evacuation and those not involved will be critical.

7.8.5 Shelter within the school

On occasions it would be inappropriate to evacuate the school community as it could be deemed safer for the students to remain within the school. Sometimes the nature of the incident will make an evacuation impossible. Several sheltering strategies are possible, for example "lockdown", sheltering in a specific refuge and segregation.

7.8.6 "Lockdown"

A lockdown is an effective means of establishing control over the school and should be the emergency procedure of choice when any "shelter" strategy is chosen. On activation of a lockdown, the school community freezes – classroom doors are secured, all students are accounted for and staff report back to the Incident Manager. Those members of the school community who are outside (playground, sports fields etc) will move to a designated location and also report back to the Incident Manager. If the lockdown was initiated due to an intruder, the Incident Manager will summon the police immediately.

Apart from establishing control over the school, one benefit of a lockdown is that, an intruder will not have access to any classroom where students are sheltering. Similarly, as there is no external movement, he cannot hide in a crowd. However, a swift response from the police is essential to limit the intrusion as quickly as possible.

The school resilience planner will need to prepare a procedure to initiate the lockdown, immediate actions for the school community on initiation of lockdown, a system to maintain the flow of information once the lockdown is in place and a system of communicating that the lockdown has been lifted.

The emergency response plan should note the procedures for the Incident Management Team and how, or if, they will meet. During an intrusion, it is more appropriate for the IMT not to leave their students, at least until the arrival of the police, as the priority must be for the staff to protect and guide the students.

On initiating lockdown, the following actions should occur:

- Staff supervising children should account for all students under their control.
- Staff supervising children should switch on mobile phones and inform the emergency point of contact:
  - o whether all students are accounted for
  - o which students are not accounted for (and where they went)
- Staff should ensure that the room is secured and that there are no suspicious bags, packages etc within the room.
- Receive briefing on the situation.
- If appropriate, members of the IMT secure their students with another class and make their way to the nominated EOC.

7.8.7 Toxic plume

In the event of an incident in the vicinity of the school – or in some cases further away - that causes a toxic or potentially toxic plume to threaten the school, and where there is no alternative guidance being provided by the emergency services or the Local Authority Schools Service, the appropriate course of action would be to bring all members of the school community inside – possibly to an identified refuge, following the guidance of, "Go in, Stay in, Tune in" and seek further guidance.

In extremis (and depending on the hazard) all external doors and windows could be shut and sealed using wet cloth or duct tape and the school community would shelter on the leeward side of the school. The IMT should liaise with the Local Authority's Schools Service or emergency services and listen to the local radio station in order to receive the latest information.

The school resilience planner should identify possible safe locations within the school. He / she should also ensure that the emergency box has a radio and spare batteries, and the plan includes a list of local radio station frequencies. The method of invoking the shelter plan should be identified in the emergency response plan, as should the detail of what the school community should do, where they should go and from where the situation will be managed.

7.8.9 Contagious illness

In the event of an incident that involves the sudden illness of one or more student and which could be contagious, the emergency plan should identify a course of action that will provide immediate medical support to the symptomatic students, whilst protecting the remainder of the school community.

The first course of action is to summon the ambulance service and get professional medical assistance. Concurrently, the group in which the symptomatic students are part of should be isolated from other students. Within that group, those who are symptomatic should be segregated. Preferably, this segregation should be in different rooms. This has two benefits - it can prevent the spread of an illness, but also, in the possible case that the illness is psychosomatic, it may prevent some students developing psychosomatic symptoms.

Normal procedures apply for summoning the ambulance service – an individual should be assigned to meet them and escort them to the scene.

It should be noted that, in the UK, if there are more than three casualties suffering from unknown symptoms, the emergency service response may be adapted. These adaptations will entail a much more complicated multi-agency response, possibly with mass decontamination equipment being erected / utilised and the involvement of the Primary Care Trust and Health Protection Agency. This extended response will cause disruption for at least the remainder of the day and / or until the cause of the illness is identified – the IMT should consider invoking the BCP.

7.8.10 Bomb threat

The school may receive a bomb threat by phone. The person receiving the call should have a bomb threat handling checklist of questions to ask and questions to answer at the end of the call. Such checklists can be found in the public domain[3]. Often the location of the device will not be known or provided. An assessment should be made by the Incident Manager as to the nature of the threat and whether it can be considered genuine. Police advice should be requested – they can advise on the most appropriate course of action and also on the possibility of secondary devices. The school resilience planner should consider speaking to the police before any incident to best prepare the bomb threat procedures.

A bomb threat - if perceived to be genuine - will require a controlled evacuation of all or part of the school. It will not be possibly simply to evacuate as per the fire drill as this may place members of the school community into closer proximity to the device and therefore in more danger. Initially, it would be appropriate to put the school into lockdown - see section 7.8.6. Note one of the suggestions for lockdown is that all teachers carry out a check of the classrooms to ensure that there are no suspicious bags or packages in the room.

If the location of the suspect device is not known – and depending on the layout of the school - then the Incident Manager or designated staff member could carry out a rapid visual assessment of the key exit routes, and if safe, use them to evacuate the school community. Otherwise it may be more appropriate to coordinate the evacuation by getting the classes out of the school by the nearest exit and then

---

3   For example, on the UK's Centre for the Protection of National Infrastruc3ture website (2009) http://www.cpni.gov.uk/Docs/Bomb_threat_checklist.pdf

making their way to the assembly area – once it has been checked and declared safe.

If the location of the suspect device is known, then the Incident Manager can control the evacuation away from it to the assembly area (bearing in mind that the assembly area may also be close to the device, in which case the alternate assembly area should be selected). In larger and well built buildings, and dependent on the size of the device, it may be appropriate to move people away from the area round the suspicious item's location, but not evacuate the entire building until the Police have checked the suspect device.

Once the school community has been evacuated, the Incident Manager should continue to liaise with the police. Specific staff from the facilities department may be requested to search the remainder of the school. Note that there may be issues with Unions regarding who can and cannot check for suspect devices. Similarly, it is not in the police remit to search for devices. Resilience planners and head teachers should consider possible solutions during the planning phase.

If the school is searched and a device has been located, the police will coordinate the management of the incident. Based on information provided and the time of day, the IMT may decide to close the school early or invoke the business continuity plan and continue critical education at a different facility.

If no device is found and the threat is confirmed to be a hoax, the Incident Manager can either conduct a more detailed search, or with advice from the police, re-enter the school and continue normal routine.

7.9 Ongoing Management of the Incident

The IMT will manage the ongoing response to an incident from an Emergency Operations Centre (EOC). On arrival at the EOC, team members should be fully briefed by the Incident Manager on the current situation. All members of the IMT should maintain a log of actions and decisions from the moment they were informed of the incident. Every member of the IMT has a specific role and should report back progress to the remainder of the IMT at regular intervals.

The IMT should make regular impact assessments (see section 7.8.1) in order to confirm the plan, allocate tasks and identify possible resources. Some of the generic tasks and issues facing the IMT include:

- Ongoing assessment of the situation and its implications.
- Ensuring the well-being of those at the scene.
- Liaising with the emergency services.
- Establishing reliable communications with staff / emergency services at the scene.
- Communicating with the school community.
- Accounting for all members of the school community at all stages of the incident.
- Ensuring the well-being of the entire school community.
- Informing the Local Authority and ongoing liaison as required.
- Informing all parents of the situation.
- Informing the parents of the injured and assisting them as required.
- Working with the Police with regards to informing parents / family of the deceased (if any).
- Managing media requests.
- Identifying relationships of victims with the school community (e.g. siblings).
- If a school trip organised by a tour operator, liaison with the tour operator.
- Business Continuity for those unaffected by the incident.
- Possible requirement for school closure (and impacts of school closure).
- Basic planning for the Recovery phase.

The template emergency response plan includes some of the detailed tasks that may be required of the IMT members in carrying out their assigned tasks. Where possible, normal business should be continued – this can be prioritised if necessary through the implementation of the Business Continuity Plan (Chapter 13). In this example, the deputy incident manager has responsibility for the school community not affected and where possible, business continuity.

The IMT should consider the possible relationships (e.g. siblings, girlfriends, boyfriends) between those involved in the incident and the remainder of the school community. If any are identified, appropriate action should be taken, depending on the level of involvement, maturity of the students and so forth. Educational psychologists should be available to provide advice. These considerations should also be made in the event of an incident affecting another school where there may be relationships with one's own school.

The IMT will need to decide whether to continue teaching or whether students should be collected and taken home. This decision may of course be taken out of the hands of the IMT if the situation dictates. The school emergency response plan will identify collection plans for when the normal collection procedure is not viable (see section 8.6).

7.10 Communicating with the School

Communications are critical to an emergency response. For an off-site emergency, the need to communicate with the scene and responders is critical and the school community needs to be kept informed as appropriate. For an on-site emergency, not only does the IMT need to communicate with the scene, but the remainder of the school community possibly need to be alerted to the hazard and both groups need to be kept informed of the ongoing situation.

The preparation phase of the planning needs to ensure that there are effective and reliable means of communicating with responders, alerting the school community to a hazard, maintaining a sufficient supply of information to both and finally ensure that contact information is available. These strategies should be reflected in the emergency response plan.

Communications with the scene are best undertaken using a telephone – either landline or mobile – and the EOC should have ample supplies of both. A useful tip is to have two phones assigned to each IMT position – one for receiving calls and the other for making them. If mobile phones are to be relied on, it is necessary to ensure that mobile phone reception is adequate and that phones have chargers.

As a minimum, two methods of alerting should be identified, both with intrinsic meaning – for example, the fire alarm will inform the school community of the need to evacuate, while the lockdown alarm will inform the school community to seek shelter following the lockdown procedure.

Having alerted the school community, the IMT will need to maintain the flow of information. Possible means of communicating to the school community include:

Alarms:
- Fire alarm pre-existing.
- Variations on this (for example, intermittent alarms) can be made to distinguish alternative responses.

Public Address System:
- Useful to pass messages to the entire school swiftly. May be heard by anyone listening. Can be drowned out by other loud noises.

Mobile phones – voice:
- Held by most teachers.
- Provides one to one communication.
- Effective, but slow to communicate with many people.
- Can be used on the move and during / following evacuation.

Mobile phones – text messaging:
- Phones held by most teachers.
- Effective way of passing short messages, quickly to a number of recipients.
- Recipient does not need to answer immediately.
- In the event of a major incident where many are expected to be using their mobile phones, there may be an overload of the mobile phone network – text messaging is more resilient to these problems.

Landline:
- Effective means for communicating one to one.
- Cost to have phones in each room.
- Static - no flexibility to move round.

Radios ("walkie-talkies"):
- May require licences.

- Reliable for passing information to other handset holders.
- Everyone can listen to conversation.
- Training required.
- Handset could be acquired and used by an intruder.
- Most handsets have limited range.

Pagers:
- Simple way to pass basic messages to multiple users – same as mobile phone, but would need to purchase pagers.
- Running costs.

E-mail:
- Rapid communication between sender and receiver.
- Requires computer access.
- Significant amount of documents and document types can be sent.
- If set up within classrooms, email provides an effective means of communicating to large numbers of recipients with minimum time delay.

School Intranet:
- Widely available information for those on the intranet network.
- One-way passage of information (publisher to recipients).
- Can take time to publish.

Internet:
- Allows information to be shared to wider audience including outside of the immediate school community – can be restricted by using secure log-ins, but needs to be set up in advance.
- One-way passage of information (publisher to recipients).
- Can take time to publish.

"Runners":
- Individual staff member moving from room to room or between individuals, passing verbal or written messages. Written communication prevents messages being corrupted.
- Requires movement outside lockdown area.
- Time consuming, especially for verbal message to all.
- Verbal message could be prone to accidental corruption.

Staff meetings:
- Used when there is no lockdown or hazard at the school.
- Updates can be provided to staff in controlled manner.
- Staff able to disseminate message to students.
- Fits into the "routine" of the school and therefore potentially more calming to the school community.

School assembly meetings:
- Used when there is no lockdown or hazard at the school.
- Updates can be provided to the entire school community in controlled manner.
- Fits into the "routine" of the school and therefore potentially more calming to the school community.

Some mechanisms are more suitable than others. For local communication, radios can be made available to teachers relatively cheaply. These also have the benefit of providing an "all-informed" means of passing information (but can have drawbacks if the wrong person gets hold of a handset). Licences may be required for radios. A public address system could be invaluable, although again, the public broadcasting of safety information during a criminal intrusion may prove to be a double-edged tactic. New technology is adapting all the time and can be used – a recent innovation is simultaneous, multiple text messaging through a provider. Teachers could each receive a text message update on the situation from the IMT (provided of course they have their mobile phones with them and switched on).

7.11 Communicating with Parents

The selected method of communicating with parents in an emergency depends on a number of variables, including whether the IMT knows who is involved, the number of children involved, the severity of the incident, the number of injuries or deceased and so forth.

Parents will be desperate for information. School resilience planners need to identify the most appropriate mechanism for their school. Direct telephone contact would be the most appropriate as this provides specific information directly to the person who needs it. However it may not be possible to get a message to individuals, so a mechanism for mass messaging may be required. Possible solutions might include the local radio station, the Internet, e-mail, answering machines that can handle multiple / simultaneous calls, SMS (multiple / simultaneous) messaging or cascade systems. It should also be remembered that not all parents will have access to the internet or e-mail, although most will now have mobile phones.

In some circumstances, for example during a school trip, it may be helpful to set up an information cascade - the emergency contact phones two people, each of whom phone two others and so on. This allows a simple message to be cascaded rapidly to all on the chain however it does have a number of problems, not least the possibility that messages can become systematically corrupted with each stage of the cascade.

Later, it may be helpful to open part of the school to parents as an information centre or for a formal briefing by the Head Teacher and the Local Authorities / School Board. This allows for the passage of information for questions to be asked (both ways) and for those requiring further support to be identified. It is personable and shows that the school management is willing to take responsibility.

Following an incident, or during a prolonged incident, one means of communicating with parents is for the head teacher to prepare a letter for the children to take to their parents, explaining the circumstances of the emergency and hopefully relieving them of any concerns.

The school website may already have a school / parents only area with restricted access. This may be utilised for "routine" communication and can be pre-loaded with useful information as part of the parent training to assist in any future emergency response. Strategies for communicating with parents and the Media are covered in more detail later (see chapters 8 and 9). The IMT must have access to emergency contact information for their school community.

7.12 Plan Appendices

The plan should include appendices to ensure that responders have all the required information and resources they need to respond. Appendices may include critical contact information, EOC location and set up procedure, media holding statements and so forth. Some examples of what may be included as an appendix are included in the template emergency response plan (in Annex A).

7.12.1 Critical contact information

The school emergency plan should include all critical contact information. As a minimum this should include the day and night time contact details for the following:

- IMT members.
- Local Authority emergency point of contact.
- Own staff.
- Governors.
- Local police station (if available).
- Local hospitals and specialist units (e.g. burns). NB Not all hospitals have Accident and Emergency departments.
- Local Primary Care Trust.
- Local GP surgery.
- Local Authority education officers.
- Local Authority Educational psychologists.
- Local Authority emergency planners.
- Local radio stations.
- Local print media.

7.12.2 IMT Emergency Operations Centre (EOC)

The emergency response plan will have identified a location from which the IMT will operate – the EOC. This location will require a number of facilities appropriate to the size of the IMT and the school. The following should be available:

- Emergency Plan – several copies.
- Telephones – sufficient for the IMT to communicate with the emergency services, local authorities, governors, parents and the media.
- Internet access – including a means of publishing information.
- E-mail access (with prepared address lists).
- Fax machine.
- Radio – to listen to local radio announcements.
- Access to a means of communicating with the school as specified in the emergency plan (PA system, radios, runners).
- Access to information on all members of the extended school community, including appropriate emergency contact information.

- Access to information on all current school trips.
- Log books – sufficient for all IMT members (see section 7.12.6).
- Meeting room - of sufficient size to include representatives of the emergency services, local authority and full IMT.
- White board or equivalent for recording key information and contact information.
- Large floor plan of the school.
- Map of the local environment.
- Media Packs.
- Student and staff emergency contact information (protected).

In reality, it is unlikely that a school will have a permanently set up facility and the equipment will need to be boxed up. The IMT and their deputies should practise setting up the EOC during exercises.

An alternate EOC location needs to be identified and prepared in case the primary EOC is inaccessible. Ideally this should be equipped the same as the primary EOC. Again, however, it is unlikely that this will be possible and the IMT will have to utilise their "emergency off-site pack" (see section 7.12.3).

The student emergency contact records (next-of-kin information) for students and staff will need to be kept available, although appropriate care needs to be taken to prevent unauthorised access. The head teacher and the deputy head should have emergency contact information available to them at all times, whether in the EOC, alternate EOC or at home.

7.12.3 IMT Emergency Off-site Pack

The IMT should prepare an emergency off-site pack in case the primary EOC is inaccessible, the alternate EOC is not equipped or the IMT is required to set up in an unprepared location. The emergency off-site pack should be stored in a separate location from the EOC – the school reception might be appropriate, as could the nominated place of safety. A second emergency off-site pack might even be prepared and kept at the nominated place of safety as a matter of course.

The emergency off-site pack should be suitably equipped to allow the IMT to manage the situation and should include the following:

- School emergency plan, including emergency contact information.
- School register – accurate for the day.
- Large scale floor plans and mapping.
- Extra floor plans and mapping for emergency services – consider having these laminated.
- Mobile phone, including mains charger and car charger.
- Analogue phones (spare).
- Emergency contact information for the school community.
- Stationery, including log book.
- List of approved collectors.
- Appropriate high-visibility clothing.
- Torches and batteries.
- Whistles.
- Loud hailer.
- Radio and batteries.
- Media Packs.

Note that the school register should be updated daily as good practice. School resilience planners should consider backing up electronic registers into a separate server or e-mailing it to a specific email address that is accessible off-site as a matter of daily routine. If the register is only kept in hard copy, then a copy should be made and stored somewhere accessible off-site (or, for example, a neighbouring building). Teachers should evacuate with a copy of their daily register.

Appropriate mapping and floor plans should be made available. The emergency services may request copies of these maps during the response, so extra copies should also be prepared and kept available in the emergency off-site pack, preferably laminated. Laminated / waterproofed copies may also be kept at reception, to be provided to the emergency services on their arrival.

7.12.4 Teacher "Grab Bags"

Teachers should each be provided with the basics for looking after their students in the event of an emergency. Ideally, this should include the following equipment:

- High-visibility tabard.
- Means of communication (mobile phone / radio) and batteries / chargers.

- Torch and batteries.
- Daily register.
- Whistle.
- Keys to the classroom.
- Relevant sections of the Emergency Plan.

7.12.5 Media Packs

The media liaison officer should prepare a media pack in advance. An electronic version of the media pack should also be available. The purpose of this pack is to provide the media with positive information on the school with minimal delay, allowing the media representatives to report to their editors / newsrooms immediately, while accurate information can be gathered and prepared for them by the media liaison officer. The media packs should be packaged professionally and should be available both from the school and from the place of safety. Electronic copies should be available.

The following items should be included in the media pack:

- General school information:
    o   Name of head teacher.
    o   Number of students.
    o   Age of students.
- Short bibliography of principal personalities.
- Current brochures.
- General information on security and emergency arrangements.
- Approved photographs of school and students.
- Recent positive media stories.
- Electronic copy of media pack (on memory stick / CD / remotely accessible server).

7.12.6 Log Books

All responders should make a log of all information received, actions taken and decisions made. Log books should be prepared in advance. The purpose of a log is to maintain a history of relevant information, messages, activities and decisions in order to enhance the response in the incident as a point of reference and as a tool to brief new appointments during a handover. Following an incident, all logs should be kept in case there is an inquiry or investigation of any form.

A log book should include the following information:

- Identity and role of the person keeping the log.
- Date and time of message, activity or decision.
- Message from (who).
- Message to (who).
- Relevant contact information.
- Message, activity undertaken or decision (with rationale).
- Signature or initials of log-keeper.

Logs can (and should) be typed up following an incident to help with the debrief process, however, as stated above, the original written logs should be kept for legal reasons.

8. RESPONSE - STRATEGIES FOR MANAGING PARENTS

Parents will rightly be desperate for information about their children and it is essential that they are kept informed honestly, accurately and in a timely manner. The plan identifies a parent liaison officer who will be responsible for all issues relating to parents (see also section 7.11). The parent liaison officer should maintain a log of all actions and specifically those parents with whom he / she has been in contact and the information provided to them.

As a matter of course, parents should have been made aware of elements of the school emergency response plan in advance of any emergency, for example, through briefings, information leaflets or publication on the website.

One of the most difficult problems facing the IMT is maintaining the most appropriate flow of information to parents whilst trying to minimise the anguish of uncertainty that may be felt by others. There will be anxiety as there may be casualties or fatalities amongst the children and the IMT may not know who they are or be allowed to inform the parents (death notification in the UK is coordinated by the Police - see section 8.3). Ironically, by efficiently providing information to some parents, those who are not informed of their child's condition might make the assumption that their child is dead. Unfortunately, as explained below, this is a situation that is difficult to avoid under the current system.

In response to an emergency and with the authorisation of the Incident Manager, the parent liaison officer should provide the following information to all parents:

- The fact that there has been an incident involving *(specify)* trip / class / entire school.
- The school is liaising with the emergency services to account for the students and staff.
- The school has activated its emergency plan.
- The school will contact parents as soon as they know any more information.
- Parents should stay near to the phone so that they can be contacted as soon as more information is known.
- More information will be made available on the local radio station (provide station name and frequency).

The purpose of this message is to inform parents that a situation has developed and to reassure them that the situation is being dealt with efficiently. It is also intended to ensure that the IMT will know how and where to get information to the parents while at the same time reassuring the parents of how they will be updated with more information.

8.1 Parents of Children Involved but Uninjured

The parents of children who have been involved, but not injured, need to be assured that their child is safe as quickly as possible. They should initially be requested to stay somewhere where they can be contacted with further information. It should not be forgotten that their child may be transported to a hospital for a check-up prior to the parents being allowed to collect him / her and that it may be at the hospital that the parents and children will be reunited.

If the emergency took place at the school, then it may be possible for this category of student to rejoin the remainder of the school, depending on the severity of the incident. However, an immediate return may not be possible – the child may still need to go to hospital for a check-up or the Police may need witness statements. Under advice from the Local Authority Educational Psychologists, the students may be recommended to attend a debriefing session. The child's parents may also decide unilaterally that their child should be collected and stay at home for the remainder of the day.

If the emergency took place on a school trip, it will be necessary to consider whether the children should remain on the school trip or whether they should return home – consideration should be made to the age of the children, their maturity, their current location and the purpose of the trip itself. Returning the children home, although it may be the natural instinct of the parents and some of the children, may not always be appropriate for all. Remember that the well-being of the children is paramount, and sometimes continuing the trip may be considered to be in the better interest of the child / young person (or even allowing some to return and others to continue).

8.2 Parents of the injured

The injured will be evacuated to hospitals by the Ambulance Service in priority order according to normal triage procedures. In a major incident, with multiple casualties, not all the injured will be taken to the same hospital as there is limited capacity in each hospital - the Ambulance Service will coordinate the distribution of casualties amongst receiving hospitals. They will – as far as practicable – have identified the casualty and recorded their names and destination. The IMT's representative at the scene should liaise with the emergency services to get this information. The Local Authority Resilience Team may also be able to assist using their contacts.

The parents of the injured should be informed that their child has been injured as soon as possible and be told to which hospital he / she has been taken. It may be necessary – and sometimes advisable – for transport to be arranged for a parent, if extremely distraught, to get to the hospital. If necessary, accommodation may also need to be organised, although there is no legal obligation to do either of these.

If the incident occurs abroad, then special measures will be required to reunite the casualty with their parents. The Local Authority may be able to assist, however this should be managed in a coordinated manner with the police and Foreign and Commonwealth Office (FCO) as the casualty may be rapidly repatriated to a hospital in the UK faster than it would take a parent to fly overseas. Management of information will be critical in such instances.

8.3 Bereaved Parents

In the UK, the Police are the designated organisation who will notify the next of kin of a fatality - not the school IMT or the Local Authority. If either the teacher at the scene or the IMT believe that they have identified any of the fatalities, they should liaise with the police and inform them of the details of the child and the parents. In some cases, the police will assign Family Liaison Officers (FLO) to bereaved parents in order to explain the identification process. These will be supported by members of the Local Authority Social Care Service if requested or required.

The fair and decent treatment of bereaved parents is of absolute importance. Unfortunately, the formal identification of fatalities is not instantaneous, especially in a mass fatality incident. The UK disaster victim identification process is designed to be precise and is intended not to allow the false identification of the deceased.

The Coroner – who has the legal responsibility for the formal identification of the deceased caused by unnatural means - will decide the final identification criteria. Post-mortem information is gathered from the scene and matched against ante-mortem information provided by witnesses, potentially including parents and teachers. When the two are matched and the identification criteria designated by the Coroner have been met, then the body can be formally identified and the bereaved can be informed. These processes directly and definitively link a physical body to a specific name – until that definitive link is made, the Coroner (and therefore the Police and School) cannot confirm that a missing individual is deceased and a parent cannot be told that their child is dead.

The Coroner is likely to reduce the identification criteria if there are fewer fatalities or if there are actual witnesses who knew the victim(s). If there is more than one victim or if the fatalities have been caused by a traumatic incident (for example, road traffic collision) then the identification criteria will be stricter and therefore the time taken to identify the deceased will be greater. However, in events where the identity of the victim is in no doubt, it is possible to adopt a less stringent and drawn-out approach.

The obvious drawback to this is that parents who know their child was involved but have not been reunited with him or her, when many other parents have been reunited with their children, will understandably fear the worst. Understanding this is critical to the management of the situation – specialist advice and practical support should be brought in from the Local Authority's Social Care service without delay.

8.4 Parents of the remainder of the school community

It is important that all parents from the school are informed of the incident – parents will certainly hear of an incident and they will want to know that the school is responding professionally and that their child is not affected. The initial parent message will provide the alert and this should be swiftly followed up with a second warning which can allay the fears of those parents whose children are not affected (although this may be intrinsic within the initial message).

Further information should be provided as required and as available. As mentioned earlier, it may be helpful to prepare an explanatory letter that can be passed to children for their parents at the end of the school day.

8.5 Reception of parents at school

Despite being requested otherwise, it is possible that parents will come to the school in the event of an emergency. Although this is not the recommended course of action, the emergency plan should identify procedures for such a situation.

Parents may come to the school under the following circumstances:

- An incident on a school trip away from the school, especially overseas where information may be limited and hospitals not immediately accessible. The school may organise centralised briefings.
- If centralised transport is being arranged to move parents to a hospital / incident location.
- An incident at the school when the parent insists that he / she comes to the school rather than wait by the phone.

For overseas emergencies, in the event that the parents of students come to the school, the emergency response plan should identify appropriate arrangements to receive and brief them. The principal reason that parents would be coming to the school in such a situation would be to receive information about what has happened and what is being done. Centralised briefings should be available from all key responders, including the Incident Manager, Governors, Local Authority senior management or School Board. Subject matter experts such as tour operators and educational psychologists may also be required to be present to answer specific questions. Parents should be advised on how they can continue to receive further information – for example, over restricted internet sites, e-mails or further regular briefings by telephone or at the school.

It may be that the parents need to be consulted on a course of action, for example, should the trip continue or should the students return home. If education is continuing, then such visits should be restricted to non-school hours in order not to disrupt the classes.

As noted in Section 8.3, special care should be taken of bereaved parents. The police should be informed of their arrival at the school, so their Family Liaison Officers can be engaged. An appropriate room should be set aside for bereaved parents in the plan. The Local Authority should also be informed in order to provide appropriate Social Care support as required. The Media may have placed themselves at the entrance to the school. Where possible, parents should be protected from them.

8.6 Collection of children by parents

The emergency plan should explain how parents should be organised to collect their children outside of normal collection hours - both from the school and from the nominated place of safety / buddy school. This may be because the school has to be closed or as a result of a general evacuation of the school premises.

When collecting from the school, normal procedures should be followed – these are known and understood by all. An alternative collection point with associated procedures needs to be prepared for the school in case that the normal location is inaccessible.

The place of safety should also have a pick-up point designated in the plan. It should be noted that the site may not be of equal size to the school, and therefore extra coordination measures may be required. The school resilience planner should visit the site, identify any limitations and plan accordingly.

A plan should also be made for those who cannot be collected until the normal working day is over (or who take the school bus at the end of the working day). The children will have to remain in the care of the school management until they can be safely collected or returned home. Consideration should also be made for those children whose parents have been evacuated from their homes to a rest centre and whose normal homeward journey has been disrupted or changed.

8.6.1 Control measures for collection

Various control measures may be required, depending on the scale of the collection, the urgency and / or the space available at the collection point.

A reliable method of accounting for children as they are collected needs to be established, especially if there has been an incident at the school.

Only nominated individuals should be allowed to collect a child. Parents should nominate approved collectors in advance and this list should be available in the IMT emergency off-site packs.

Depending on the size of the school and other factors, it may be advisable to stagger the collection. It may be necessary to allocate a timeframe for each school class.

Although parents may be told about the emergency collection plan arrangements in advance, it will still be necessary to confirm the actual plan on the day.

9. RESPONSE - STRATEGIES FOR MANAGING THE MEDIA

There is likely to be a great deal of media interest in any school incident, sadly, especially if it involves fatalities, casualties or a school intrusion. Media interest may come from local, national and international media companies.

The emergency response plan needs to designate a media liaison officer who will be responsible for all matters relating to the media during an incident. Ideally, this individual should receive media training and should have had some prior contact with the Local Authority's communications team and hopefully the local police Press Relations Officers. A media assistant will almost certainly be required to support the media liaison officer.

Although the head teacher, as Incident Manager, may decide to make statements to the media, he / she should not be the primary point of contact. The duty of the head teacher is to manage the incident and therefore he / she needs to maintain an overview of the entire situation and not focus on one aspect, especially one which, though important for reputational issues, is a distraction from the principal task of managing the incident and protecting the school community. Member(s) of the governing body may also be used as a media spokesperson in support of the designated media liaison officer.

The Local Authority communications teams should be involved in the response as they will be able to provide professional support to the school. They are able to provide advice for the media liaison officer and could deploy a communications officer to assist either at the scene, the school, or perhaps both if required.

However, there are other reasons why the Local Authority communications teams need to be involved. In an incident, multi-agency plans foresee that the police will coordinate the media strategy – the Local Authority Communications team will be liaising with the police and will be able to provide this strategy to the school media liaison officer. This ensures that all organisations send out the same key messages. Similarly, as the school employer, the Local Authority will also wish to ensure that the messages being sent to the Media reflect their perspective.

During the initial stages of the emergency, there may be a paucity of information. This will not stop the media putting pressure on the school to provide information.

The media liaison officer will require access to at least two telephones and should have at least one assistant, also with two phones. A computer with access to e-mails and the Internet should be provided, preferably with a means of publishing information. As with all members of the IMT, the media liaison officer will need to keep a log of his / her actions. Contact details of the local radio stations and media outlets should be included in the school emergency plan.

The media may gather outside the school – they should not be allowed onto school property. Where possible they should be gathered at a pre-arranged 'media information point' – a location identified by the planner that will not interfere with the emergency response or school matters, but from where they can film appropriate footage of the school. It will be necessary to look after the media and provide them with regular updates – they should be told when these will occur and where possible updates should be provided to tie in with the major transmission schedules. The media liaison officer should coordinate this, possibly in conjunction with the police press relations officer, if they are present.

If statements are made to the media, they should be supported with written copies.

A media centre for press conferences should be identified in advance. This can be done in liaison with the emergency services and Local Authority communications team. This should be located off school property in order not to interfere with the children still at the school. The facility should have a conference room which can cater for a large number of journalists. There should be sufficient parking for the Media's TV vehicles.

The media may attempt to call the school on any phone line in order to gain an "exclusive". All calls should be directed to the media liaison officer using a prepared script. If the media liaison officer is overwhelmed, this is a sign that support should be sought from the Local Authority. Pooling journalists may be an appropriate means of providing reports – again, advice should be sought from the Local Authority.

For situations where children who have been involved in an emergency are returning from an overseas trip, the Media may be interested in their arrival. Care should be taken to protect the children and parents from unwanted media intrusion. It may be appropriate - and possibly desired by those groups - to meet the media on their own terms. If this is the case the children and parents should receive a briefing in advance by an experienced press officer and then be allowed to meet the media. Supervision would be required to protect the children if the questioning becomes too traumatic.

10. RESPONSE & RECOVERY - STRATEGY FOR SCHOOL CLOSURE

Although the final decision for school closure rests with the head teacher, advice should be taken from the local authority schools service / School Board. Possible reasons for closing the school following an incident could include:

- Quarantine.
- Forensic investigation.
- Clean-up.
- Sanitisation / decontamination.
- Redecoration following an incident.
- Reconstruction.
- Allowing the school community to come to terms with a traumatic emergency.
- Insufficient staff to maintain appropriate ratio of staff to children.

Even if there has been no physical damage to the school infrastructure, the emergency may have been too traumatic for students to return immediately to their studies. Likewise, parents might demand to keep their children at home. The head teacher will need to consult teachers, parents, the governing body and the local authority / employer in order to decide what is most appropriate in the circumstances.

If the school needs to be shut for a short period of time, then there is unlikely to be a significant impact on the children's education and they should be able to stay at home. However, consideration should be given to parents who are unable to take time off work to look after their children during the working day – some level of support may be required, and assistance might be sought from the Local Authority Schools Service or Youth Service.

The school will need to invoke its BCM plans (see chapter 13), especially if the incident occurs at a critical time during the school year. For example, if the emergency occurs during exams, consideration should be made as to delaying them while arrangements can be made. If the exams in question are national examinations, then the head teacher will need to make appropriate arrangements, possibly with other schools, for the students to take the exams. The head teacher will also need to consult the Examination Boards in order to alert the Boards to the incident and the students affected.

Even if the incident did not occur at a critical time of the year, schools have a statutory duty to continue education and therefore they will need to have plans and business continuity strategies in place to ensure this. Further information on BCM can be found in chapter 13.

If the school cannot be opened within a reasonable period of time, the head teacher will have to consult with the local authority schools service / employer to arrange alternative accommodation for the students for the duration of the closure – possibly even another school. Appropriate logistical arrangements will also have to be made, for example, transport to get the children to the receiving school. Whereas, state schools will have a wider choice of appropriate schools available, independent schools should consider making mutual support arrangements in advance.

In the event of a temporary movement of children to another school, consideration should be made to the reception of those children in the new classes, especially if the incident was traumatic. For further information on the Recovery, see chapter 11.

Any period of closure may also be utilised by the school management to make plans for the reopening of the school and the management of the recovery phase. These plans should be made in conjunction with the local authority schools service and educational psychologists, as well as parents, teachers and the governing body. The time may also be used to train staff in how to identify possible warning signs of psychological injury.

Practically, any period of closure should also be considered as a possible opportunity in the event that decoration, renovation or refurbishment had been planned. Such an opportunity should not however be allowed to detract from the primary purpose of educating children.

Note also, that the unnecessary continued closure of a school may have a wider community impact, as parents – who may be critical workers in the community like fire fighters, nurses and police officers – will have to remain at home to look after their children, thus depriving their employers of their services and putting pressure on those critical organisations.

Depending on the incident itself, the reopening of the school may be formalised with a ceremony / school assembly. Consideration should be given to students being allowed time to get used to being back in the school before moving straight into class – especially as some of the students may not have seen each other since the incident itself.

Throughout any closure of the school – and indeed throughout the entire emergency – the school management should pay particular attention to keeping the parents informed of the situation and where necessary, involved in the decision-making.

11. RECOVERY STRATEGIES

The recovery phase of an emergency follows the response phase, although there may be some overlap – basic planning for the recovery should begin during the response itself. Generally, the response phase ends when the casualties have been taken to hospital, the emergency services have left the scene, children are with their parents and there is no longer a threat to life.

The management of the recovery will be a long process, the actual length of which will vary depending on the emergency. Injuries sustained may be both physical and psychological. For the latter, the IMT should maintain a very close working relationship with the educational psychologists assigned by the Local Authority. Note that, despite the difficulty of managing large numbers, victims should be treated as individuals.

There may be a number of issues that need to be considered during the recovery phase, including:

Identification of Victims:
- Physically injured and their rehabilitation.
- Possibility of trauma to those directly involved.
- Indirect victims suffering psychological trauma.

Practical Support:
- Practical needs of the victims, depending on their injury.
- Practical support to the families – financial, legal, administrative, social care.

Emotional Support:
- Management of unofficial / spontaneous memorials and gifts.
- Funerals.
- Memorial Services.

Management of memories.
- Anniversaries.
- Impact of outside world, e.g. media pressure, public inquiry.

Structural:
- Structural damage to the school infrastructure or facilities.
- Damage to school equipment or property.
- Sanitisation, decontamination or demolition of school facilities.
- Restoration, refurbishment and re-equipping of school.
- Reopening of school.

Other considerations:
- Business Continuity for remainder of school.
- Legal – e.g. public inquiry.
- Disaster funds and their management.

11.1 Management of the physically injured

The health services will be directly responsible for those who have been injured in the incident and will manage their physical recovery. The physical recovery may take time and it is possible that the casualties may never fully recover. The school will need to take these injuries into consideration as it would any other injury or disability.

The school community will need to be actively involved in the reintegration of the injured back into the school – consider how the school community will welcome back a child who has suffered a traumatic amputation. The children may not return at the same time, which may make "moving on" difficult for the remaining children as they may be regularly reminded of the incident. As discussed below, the impact of the incident on those not directly affected should be carefully monitored by staff and parents.

11.2 Management of those psychologically injured

The management of those with actual or potential psychological injuries is more difficult due to the lack of visible physical injury. However, it should be remembered that these injuries – if untreated – could have a significant negative impact on a child and his / her family for the remainder of that child's life. The local authority employs professional educational psychologists who are available to advise and assist head teachers in making appropriate plans to care for those with psychological injury.

Educational psychologists should be assigned to the school by the Local Authority – if not they should be requested. In general they should be used to advise the IMT about how best to manage the psychological recovery of the students (and help with the remainder of the extended school community - adult social care assistance can also be sought through the Local Authority). Educational psychologists can train members of the school staff in the identification of the warning signs of psychological injury and advise on the most appropriate actions if such symptoms appear, potentially taking more direct action if the head teacher and parents agree. They may also be used in schools with older students to brief the students directly, possibly at an Assembly, by classes, or in smaller groups.

Identifying those who are at risk from psychological injury is not always a simple task, and the school management need to be aware and prepare for cases they may not have otherwise anticipated. It should be remembered that psychological injuries will not necessarily manifest themselves immediately and therefore a member of the school community may appear unaffected initially. Staff, parents and fellow students should be told of the possible signs and symptoms of psychological injury, and that a significant number of those involved - and some not directly involved - may be affected to some degree. They should know what to do if they recognise the symptoms in themselves or others.

The school management should also be aware of the indirect victims amongst the school community - consideration should be made to siblings, girlfriends, boyfriends, classmates and team-mates of those injured or killed, uninvolved staff members and the parents. Other indirect victims may even include those who have been involved in an incident before and whose latent memory has been re-awakened due to this latest trauma. Thought should also be paid to how the incident may impact the parents and family of those involved as this too may have a negative impact on the children. Note that a school that was not directly affected by an incident may find that one of its students is connected to the emergency, for example, through a sibling.

Throughout, the local authority social care services and schools service will be able to provide access to appropriate assistance (social workers, educational psychologists, bereavement counsellors etc) through their post-disaster support team (or equivalent).

Various strategies and principles that might be considered by school management include:

- Treating those affected as individuals, not just a group of victims.
- Training the wider school community in recognising the signs and symptoms of psychological injury.
- Allowing an educational psychologist the opportunity to visit classes and become a "familiar sight" to the students – but not an imposition.
- Allowing students to identify a member of staff with whom they feel comfortable.
- Provision of suitable "quiet rooms" where those affected can be comfortable and reflect, away from the school routine.
- Support the students' own measures for dealing with the incident, such as through the establishment of a club.
- When possible due to the maturity of the children, allow the children to manage the level of support they require.
- Consider how the incident may have impacted on the parents (an issue for local authority social care) that may manifest itself through a student.
- Manage the impact on teachers – both those involved in the incident and / or the recovery.

11.3 Recovery Considerations - Fatalities

Special consideration may be required for traumatic incidents involving fatalities or serious injuries amongst the school community, regardless of whether the school remains open or closes temporarily. The impacts may vary from school to school or between age groups, and the IMT will need to consult with an educational psychologist as well as those who know the students – and possibly the students themselves – in order to determine the most appropriate course of action.

Possible issues that may occur include:

- Managing the spontaneous memorials that may appear at or near the school.
- Removing the names of the deceased from the school register.
- Clearing out lockers of the deceased and reallocation of locker space.
- Rearranging the seating plan in the classrooms.
- Reassigning members of groups.
- Managing the first assemblies.
- Consideration should be paid to subjects being studied – might they raise unwanted emotions.
- When to remove flowers and what to do with them.
- When to remove other memorials (candles, pictures, toys etc) and what to do with them.
- Memorial services – when to hold them, who should attend.
- Funeral services – who to attend; care for those attending. (Also depends on the family of the deceased).
- Managing key dates in the school / public mind (one week on) and anniversaries.
- Managing the possibly continuing Media interest in the event; managing emotions following similar events elsewhere.
- Managing the impact of associated events – for example, the start or completion of a public enquiry.

A fine line needs to be drawn between wrapping the children in cotton wool – which potentially they may not want or need – and exacerbating the trauma they have already undergone. Although the school will have to make generic plans for the recovery, those who are suffering must be treated as individuals.

It is noted that the impact of an emergency may be long-term and can last for years. Although for a school there will be a moving on of the survivors as children grow older and leave, memories and anniversaries will remain with the victims and the school may continue to be the focus for these memories.

11.4 Continuation of Education

Where possible, those not directly involved in the incident will continue their education under the school business continuity plan. For the victims, however, there may be a pause in learning while they recover. Generally speaking, this should be kept to a minimum however expert advice will need to be sought from the educational psychologists.

The continuation of education for the victims is important and must be managed intelligently, coherently and with consideration. A management plan should be prepared by the Head Teacher that balances the need for education against the emotional recovery of the children. Indeed, the return to full-time education could be seen as a critical element in the emotional recovery. Throughout this period, the head teacher and staff will have to bear in mind the considerations raised earlier regarding the management of those with physical and psychological injuries, and should consult the educational psychologists to get a professional view on how appropriate is the proposed education plan.

Once again, BCM is a critical issue here and the invocation of the BCP, possibly under the direction of the Deputy Incident Manager, should be considered at the earliest appropriate opportunity, in order to ensure that the process of education for the majority of students is continued.

11.5 Disaster Funds

Following previous disasters involving schools, the reaction of the public has been to send money or gifts. The receipt of gifts poses some logistical problems that will need to be carefully managed. However, the management of disaster funds raises legal and accountancy issues, such as tax relief on charities and identifying who is entitled to receive the funds, or not. The British Red Cross Society has a Disaster Appeal Scheme[4] that can be accessed through the Local Authority or directly to them. Without the resources for accountants and without other expertise, it is generally better to bring in this Charity to help facilitation of the Fund.

---

4   British Red Cross Disaster Appeal Scheme [2009] http://www.redcross.org.uk/standard.asp?id=82677

12. TRAINING, EXERCISING, MAINTAINING AND REVIEW

All those with a role in the school emergency response plan should receive some form of training so that they fully understand their roles and how they interface with others. Some IMT members will be nominated deputies and these people should also receive training in both roles. Training should be held at least annually and the IMT should always have the latest copy of the plan.

Where appropriate, such as with fire drills and lockdown drills, children should also receive training. Parents should be provided with enough information so they know what will happen and what is expected of them during an emergency. Information materials should be kept up to date.

Some members of staff will require specific role training – for example the media liaison officer will be required to undergo media training. Ideally, all staff should receive basic first aid training (those acting as trip / activity leaders away from the school should definitely receive this). Where appropriate, students may be encouraged to undertake basic first aid training – after all, this can only be beneficial in future life. Recognising the signs of psychological trauma was noted earlier as a useful skill in the event of an emergency – like first aid, this is a life skill that might be taught to staff and older children regardless of the existence of an incident.

Exercises are a means of confirming the training and understanding of the individuals / teams. It is an opportunity to work together, to talk through possible scenarios and to validate the plan. Feedback can be used to revise the plan to make it more effective.

Exercises can come in two basic forms – 'tabletop' and 'live'. A tabletop exercise is a useful format as it combines flexibility, simplicity, speed and economy. Those being exercised can sit around a table (or possibly, a 'virtual' table) and are presented with a scenario which develops as the group make decisions. 'Injects' (updates to the scenario that are 'injected' into the group discussions) are provided by the exercise planner who wishes to test various elements of the plan or group's capability.

A 'live' exercise takes more time and resources to prepare and coordinate. Often these require support from other organisations to make it realistic. It 'acts out' the scenario in real time and the responders actually do their tasks for real, not simply explain what they would do under the circumstances (as per the tabletop exercise). So, for example, the IMT would meet in the alternate EOC location, following an evacuation and would have to see whether they have what they require in their 'emergency off-site pack'. The media liaison officer would need to prepare a media statement and possibly go through a press conference scenario, while the parent liaison officer might have to keep a group of parents informed of the situation.

Some example scenarios for a tabletop exercise are included in Annex C.

The school emergency response plan should be maintained on a regular basis. Contact information should be updated as it happens. As a minimum the plan should be reviewed annually, when there have been significant changes to the school or when an exercise or real incident have identified where revisions should be made. The requirement for training, exercising, review and maintenance should be stated in the school health and safety policy (section 3.4).

The school emergency plan should be dated and have version control to ensure that all responders have the latest copy of the plan.

13. BUSINESS CONTINUITY MANAGEMENT

Business Continuity Management (BCM) is a management process that seeks to ensure that an organisation – in this case, the school – is capable of maintaining its critical activities in the event of a disruptive challenge.

The difference between the BCM programme and the emergency response plan is that the latter is focussed on responding to an emergency, "to save life and prevent further injury to the school community in the event of a potentially life-threatening emergency", whilst BCM is focussed on maintaining the continuation of identified critical activities – there may not be, or have been, a direct threat to life or limb. Elements of BCM can also be utilised following the activation of the emergency response plan in order to continue the fundamental activities of the school.

BCM is intended to ensure the continuation of those critical activities that are absolutely critical to a business's survival. Unlike risk management, it will drill down to identify these specific activities and then focus on them to provide plans that will ensure the continuation - or priority recovery - of them.

There is a British Standard (BS-25999)[5] that can guide an organisation through six identified stages of planning. The phases are:

1. BCM Programme Management.
2. Understanding the Organisation.
3. Determining BCM strategy.

---

5   British Standards Institution (2006). BS25999-1:2006. British Standards Institution.

4. Developing and implementing BCM response.
5. Exercising, maintaining and reviewing.
6. Embedding BCM in the organisation's culture.

The school health and safety policy (section 3.4) should include a section on BCM arrangements. This section should state the requirement for a BCM Programme and its scope. It should confirm the full support of the School Board / Employers and management. It should also note any key policy items, such as that all contracts with external providers should require verified and effective BCM plans to be held by the providers.

13.1 BCM Programme

A template BCM programme for a school is included at Annex B. The BCM Programme should be approved by the school management, employer and Governors.

The BCM Programme provides the framework around which the end product – the business continuity plan – is based. (Note however, that this remains an iterative process, and that the Programme will also detail a maintenance and review programme). The programme will define the programme management structure, including roles, oversight and responsibilities. A BCM planner must be identified as should a senior manager or governor to provide oversight of the programme.

The BCM programme defines several key elements that will provide the basis for analysis during the later stages of the Programme implementation phases. These key elements are:

- The criteria identifying what constitutes a critical activity.
- The time scales for the Recovery Time Objectives (RTOs).
- The impact scale for the Business Impact Analysis (BIA).
- Criteria for identifying Mission Critical Activities (MCAs).
- The risk consequences against which the MCAs will be assessed.
- The minimum requirements for the Business Continuity Plan.
- Training, exercising, maintenance and review details.

13.2 Understanding the Organisation

The second phase of the BCM process is designed to analyse the organisation and can be divided into three phases – the Business Impact Analysis (BIA), a resource assessment and a risk review. The output from this phase is to determine the school's Mission Critical Activities (MCAs) and to place them in a priority order for restoration, to identify the basic resources required to undertake the critical activity and to assess vulnerabilities that may be caused by specific hazards and where possible to identify Business Continuity strategies that can be used to mitigate a hazard / threat.

13.2.1 Business Impact Assessment

The first task is to confirm the generic activities that the school undertakes. This might be taken from the school's equivalent of a business plan. Possible activities that could be included are:

- Education of specific year groups.
- School examinations.
- National tests / examinations.
- School management.
- Theatre trips.
- Outdoor activity trips (e.g. canoeing, mountaineering).
- Emergency response.

Knowing these activities, it is possible to compare them against a list of critical activity criteria to determine which of the school's generic activities are critical. Critical activity criteria should be listed in the BCM Programme (Section 13.1) and could include:

- When the loss of the activity will result in a hazard to life and limb.
- When the loss of the activity will result in a failure to provide a statutory duty.
- When the loss of the activity will result in severe reputational damage to the employer or the school.
- When the loss of the activity will result in a financial loss to the employer or the school.
- When an activity is designated as a critical activity for the employer or other key stakeholder.

Examples of likely critical activities for the school would be the ability to respond to an emergency and the continuation of examinations. Other critical activities may also be identified.

Having identified the critical activities it is necessary to determine how quickly each activity needs to be restored to its minimum level – the Recovery Time Objective (RTO) – and for how long can the critical activity be discontinued without causing a catastrophic failure – this is known as the Maximum Tolerable Period of Disruption (MTPD). The faster the requirement to recover the activity, then the higher the priority of the activity should be on the recovery checklist. For example, the capability to respond to an emergency should be immediate, so it must have a high place on the recovery list.

Timeframes should be identified in the BCM Programme (section 13.1) and may be:

- Immediate.
- Between 1 - 2 hours.
- Within 24 hours.
- Within the week.
- Between one week and one month.
- Over one month

Finally, it is necessary to determine the impact if that activity did not take place. A possible scale, with associated definitions to assist BC planners (section 13.1) could be:

- **Intolerable** – the loss of this activity would have an unacceptable impact on the school.
- **High** – the loss of this activity would have a severe impact on the school, but provided this is effectively managed and rapidly restored it is bearable.
- **Medium** - the loss of this activity would have an impact on the school and will need to be restored, but the loss would be bearable for a while and its restoration would not be the highest priority.
- **Low** – the loss of this activity would have a minimal impact on the school.
- **Negligible** – the loss of this activity would not have an impact on the school.

For example, although not desirable, a short delay might be acceptable for school examinations, however it would be intolerable for students to miss national examinations. Note that the impact on some activities may initially be tolerable, but if left for over a certain period of time, this would become intolerable. For example, the closure of schools for a fortnight during the term because of a flu pandemic may be tolerable, but for over two weeks the impact may become intolerable. This is where the Maximum Tolerable Period of Disruption (MTPD) is important.

Having identified the critical activities, how quickly they must be continued, after how long the loss becomes unbearable, and finally understood what would be the impact if the activity was not undertaken, it is possible to determine which critical activities need to be planned for – i.e. the Mission Critical Activities (MCAs) - and of those, what is the priority order for restoration. The BCM Programme should identify the criteria for determining the MCAs (section 13.1). The criteria could be:

- Any critical activity with an intolerable impact.
- Any activity with an immediate, 1-2 hours or under 1 day RTO.
- Any activity with a high impact and an RTO of less than one week.
- Any activity with a high impact and an MTPD of less than one month.

The end product may see a list of Mission Critical Activities with accompanying Recovery Time Objectives as below:

- Emergency response capability – immediate.
- Continuation of national examinations (GCSE) – within 24 hours.
- Continuation of education – within 1 week.

13.2.2 Resource Assessment

A resource assessment needs to be conducted for each Mission Critical Activity in order to ascertain what resources are required to undertake that specific activity both at normal and minimal level. Resources could be considered under the following headings (with examples):

People.
- Who.
- How many.
- Doing what.
- Training / qualifications required.
- Legal requirements (e.g. CRB check).

Facilities.
- Locations (where; keys; key-holders).
- Type of facility required.
- Home-working possible.
- "Hot-desking" possible.
- Emergency Operations Centre.

Equipment.
- General equipment (books; stationery; workstations).
- Specialist equipment (science equipment).
- Transport (specialist; group; car).

Information Technology.
- Hardware (computers and office ancillaries; servers; networks; back-up mechanisms).
- Software.

Communications.
- Telephony (landline; mobile phones; faxes; pagers).
- IT based (email; intranet; extranet; internet; wi-fi; mobile broadband).
- Other (radios; PA systems; TV; local radio stations).

Information.
- Paper archives.
- Documents (exam papers; answer papers; business continuity plans).
- Records (contact information; next of kin information; previous results).
- Electronic archives.
- Passwords.

Critical interdependencies.
- Suppliers / providers of services (e.g. catering).
- Recipients of services.
- Other schools / organisations.

Other.
- For example, key dates / seasonal nature of the activity (national exams).

There are a number of outputs from the resource assessment. As the name suggests, it identifies what resources are required to maintain the Mission Critical Activity at the minimal and normal levels. It may identify any weaknesses or vulnerabilities in the current status – for example, where two people are required to manage a task, only one is sufficiently qualified, or a single point of failure. It will also identify where there is a critical reliance on a specific service provider who may be outside the direct control of the school – for example, a catering company. If that caterer is required for a Mission Critical Activity, then the caterer must be required to have an effective Business Continuity Plan of their own. This must be written into their contract and checked.

As weaknesses or vulnerabilities are identified, the BC planner needs to identify solutions to those problems. These could be solutions that can be implemented proactively – such as the caterer preparing a BCP and the staff member gaining a qualification. Similarly, the solution might be one that can only be implemented following the invocation of the BCP, for example, calling in mutual aid from another school (although an agreement and mechanism to this effect could be agreed in advance)

To summarise, at the end of this stage, the BC planner will know what resources are required to continue the Mission Critical Activity at its most basic level and what are required to run at the normal level. At the same time, the BC planner will have a list of proactive actions that are required to be undertaken and a list of reactive strategies that can be included in the BCP.

13.2.3 Risk Review

Following the resource assessment, a risk review should be undertaken for each Mission Critical Activity. The purpose of this review is to understand how the consequences of hazards might impact on the Mission Critical Activity. To do this it is necessary to understand that, although there may be a large number of hazards, the consequences of those hazards may be the same (for example, losing access to a facility could be the result of a fire, a gas leak, a criminal activity, a bomb threat or floods). Essentially, it is the consequence of the hazard, not the hazard itself that matters to a BC planner.

The UK Government[6] has provided a list of generic consequences (that has been enhanced to include loss of IT) which are considered to cover a wide range of possible threats and hazards. These are:

- Large scale temporary absence of staff – up to 35% over a 2-3 week period (relating to the 2008 UK Government flu pandemic planning criteria. Figures could be adjusted appropriately).
- Permanent or long-term loss of staff – through death / serious injury.
- Denial of site or geographical area.
- Loss of mains electricity.
- Disruption to transport.
- Loss of mains water and sewerage.
- Loss of availability of oil and fuel – disruption for up to 10 days.
- Loss of gas - short term losses to localities; restored within days. (May also cause 3 hour electricity power rotations).
- Loss of electronic communications.
- Loss of IT (server and / or IT equipment or software).

The BC planner should consider each consequence and Mission Critical Activity in turn, identifying what the impact would be and what measures could be taken to mitigate these impacts. For example, loss of access to the school may have a significant impact on sitting national exams, so an alternative arrangement will need to be identified. Again, these measures may be both useful for identifying proactive solutions or may be used reactively to form the basis of the BC strategies that in turn will help build the BCP.

---

6   Directgov Preparing for Emergencies (2009) http://www.direct.gov.uk/en/Governmentcitizensandrights/Dealingwithemergencies/Preparingforemergencies/DG_176599

Sometimes it may be necessary to focus on a specific hazard or threat that has been identified in advance, for example, the prospect of a flu pandemic or Teacher's Union strike. Although most of the consequences would be covered by the list there may be some details that could be considered and strategies that can be formulated for this specific event.

The output of the risk review is the identification of suitable strategies that could mitigate the consequences of a number of hazards or threats. These will be the basis of any BCP. For example, to counter the possible loss of school premises, the planner would perhaps identify alternate locations (such as a "buddy school") but for any longer period of time other strategies might need to be considered, such as methods of remote working from home or liaising with the local authority's schools service to provide temporary accommodation elsewhere.

13.3 Determining the BCM Strategy

However, before the business continuity planning begins in earnest, it is necessary to identify the strategic risk treatment strategy for each Mission Critical Activity, bearing in mind cost, resources, planning, etc. Although weaknesses and vulnerabilities may have been identified there may be circumstances (for example, cost, complexity or time) whereby the school may decide not to continue the business continuity planning process.

As noted in section 3.3, there are four possible risk treatment strategies available to the management. These are:

- Tolerate.
- Transfer.
- Terminate.
- Treat.

It may be that the strategies required to continue the service identified in the 'Understanding the Organisation' phase are so unacceptable (for example, expensive) that the head teacher may decide to accept the risk without a contingency strategy - tolerate. The head teacher may decide to transfer the risk, possibly through a contractual arrangement. If the risk is so great it may be more appropriate to terminate the risk (by ceasing to provide that particular service (again, an unlikely outcome for a school). The remaining activities will be treated with the preparation of contingency plans.

Where "treat" is the chosen risk treatment, the business continuity planner should utilise the operational BC strategies already identified in the resource assessment and risk review. If the BC planner has all the resources available to continue the process then he should move on to the next phase. However, he may need to approach the school management in order to acquire strategic resources, funds or authorisation to implement specific operational strategies, such as requesting the head teacher to discuss a mutual aid arrangement with another local school.

13.4 Developing and implementing a BCM response

Phase four of BS:25999 considers the preparation of the Business Continuity Plan (BCP) itself. The BCP should utilise the same incident management structure as the school emergency response plan – this prevents duplication and ensures simplicity. Annex B provides a template checklist of items required in a BCP.

As with the school emergency response plan, the BCP will need to be simple, logical and easy to apply. In the event of an invocation, it will detail who does what, how, with what, where (or where else), when and to what purpose. These details should be derived directly from the earlier planning – the resources required to continue a Mission Critical Activity are detailed in the resource assessment and the various strategies required to mitigate an incident type are found in the risk review.

The BCP focuses on ensuring that those Mission Critical Activities that have been identified as critical to the survival of the school will be continued. During an invocation of the BCP, strategic management (the IMT) should ensure that these do continue and where necessary, allocate staff and resources from other areas to ensure continuation of service. Again, as with the school emergency response plan, the IMT will need to meet regularly to receive feedback from staff and react accordingly.

Although the BCP will ensure that sufficient physical resources are present with which to manage a BCP invocation, it should include a section where specific contingencies are provided for specific issues. Some of these contingency strategies may be those identified during the risk review, but others may be derived from previous experience, including previous invocations.

For example, the review of the risk of managing a large scale (35%) temporary (between 2-3 weeks) absence of staff (based on the realistic worst case scenario for a flu pandemic would have identified a number of possible contingencies that the IMT would consider implementing, including possible closure. In such a case, the BC planner would record possible contingency strategies that might be utilised by the IMT, such as use of the school internet site for providing school tasks, a central group email address for staff receiving completed tasks, focussing on specific year groups with remaining staff, working with other schools to "share" teacher resources, and so forth. Not all the contingencies have to be used for a specific issue, but it provides the IMT with a list of possible actions so they have the luxury of not having to respond to an incident completely from scratch.

It should be remembered that the BCP will focus on continuing Mission Critical Activities. Despite this, all departments should attempt to continue their normal activities only dropping these when required to by the IMT who will be trying to ensure that the high priority Mission Critical Activities receive all the resources required to continue, possibly at the expense of other activities. A template checklist for teams without Mission Critical Activities is also included in Annex B.

Similarly, the BCP should also provide a list of all other non-Mission Critical Activities that need to be recovered once the Mission Critical Activities are functioning and resources remain to recover more. This list of activities should be prioritised into relative importance (based on the Business Impact Analysis), the required speed of recovery (based on the identified Recovery Time Objectives) or the Maximum Tolerable Period of Disruption (MTPD).

13.5 Exercising, maintaining and reviewing BCM arrangements

As per the emergency plan, the BCM arrangements need to be known and understood. Training will be required, complemented with exercises – either tabletop or live play – on an annual basis. Feedback from the exercises (and training) should be used to validate the plan and where necessary improve it. The plan should be reviewed on a regular basis – at least annually or when there have been significant changes to the school's structure, administration or organisation.

13.6 Embedding BCM in the organisation's culture

Ideally, BCM would be deeply embedded in the culture of the organisation. In reality, all staff should be aware of the emergency response procedures and the IMT should be aware of the BCM strategies. The IMT's participation in BCM training and exercises should see the appropriate level of BCM awareness.

Looking outwards, the school should ensure that all suppliers and external providers of services have Business Continuity Plans in place – this is best practice for all service providers, not simply those that support Mission Critical Activities.

14. CONCLUSION

The aim of this book is to provide school resilience planners with practical guidance on emergency management and business continuity management for schools in order that they can prepare a school emergency response plan and a school business continuity plan.

The similarities and differences between emergency management, as exemplified by the six phases of Integrated Emergency Management (IEM), and business continuity management are seen in the aim of each. The former aims to ensure that the school is able to respond to an incident that threatens the life or health of one or more members of the school community, or the school property or environment. The latter aims to ensure that the school can continue its critical activities (that have been identified in the BCM process) in the event of a disruption to the school's routine functioning. There are crossovers in each.

During the anticipation stage of IEM, it has been seen that although there is no specific legal duty to have a school emergency response plan or business continuity plan, the relationship between a state school and the local authority places an implied duty on the school management under the Civil Contingencies Act (2004).

The assessment phase considers for which hazards or threats the school needs to prepare emergency response plans and ensures that the school health and safety policy reflects the requirement for resilience planning. It also analyses what other resources are already available to the school resilience planner. Each of the hazards or threats are individually analysed in the preparation phase to create contingency strategies that will be collated and eventually incorporated into the school emergency response plan.

The preparation phase also ensures that the practical preparations required for the response, such as training or the identification and equipping of an EOC, are undertaken. The prevention phase occurs concurrently to the preparation phase, both enhancing the resilience of the school. Preventative measures can include structural and security enhancements.

The response phase for the school is substantiated in the successful implementation of the school emergency response plan. The recovery phase looks at the longer term impacts of the incident, once the initial response is completed. These impacts could include physical and psychological injury to members of the school community or structural damage to the school facilities.

The requirement for business continuity management in the school should be written into the school health and safety policy and should follow a specific programme. This BCM programme will formalise the analysis of the school's activities in order to identify which are Mission Critical, and will then analyse these to create specific strategies for continuing them based on a prioritised recovery timetable. Eventually, as with the emergency response plan, the school business continuity plan will collate all appropriate strategies and resources to ensure that those Mission Critical Activities can be continued in the event of a disruption. The plan will use the same management structure as the emergency response plan.

School emergencies are inevitable – what is not known are to which school, how severe or where they will occur. Other truisms are that no two incidents will ever be the same and no plan will ever exactly match the circumstances of the incident. A school emergency response plan is expected to ensure that the school's IMT is best placed to respond flexibly to the incident – the management will still have to use their initiative, common sense and understanding of the emergency response and business continuity plans.

Finally, some incidents appear to be so extreme and unstoppable, such as in the face of a determined assault (for example, Beslan, Columbine, Dunblane) that it would seem that a simple emergency response plan would not suffice. This is not true. First, these types of emergency are rare. The majority of emergencies are far smaller (although to those affected, the comparison of impact is

not a relevant factor) and are certainly manageable throu.
implementation of a prepared plan. Secondly, although casualt.
the extreme events may be inevitable, the competent manageme
of that which can be managed, in the circumstances, may save lives.
Furthermore, the importance of training comes to the fore – the
school community, trained in the emergency response plan would
know what to do in the event of an incident and using their initiative
and skills (including first aid training) would respond according to
the situation.

The ability to respond to a school emergency is essential as part of
a school's responsibility to its community, its reputation and in the
case of independent schools, possibly their survival. The impact of
not having a plan could have potentially devastating consequences
to the children and staff, possibly for the rest of their lives.

Ultimately, resilience planning is not just a matter of fulfilling legal
obligations – it is about managing the risk to the quality of life and
future life of the children, staff and wider community of a school,
protecting them from harm and ultimately ensuring that the school
is able to undertake its primary function – deliver education to its
children in a safe, learning environment.

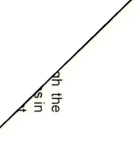

Annex A - School Emergency Response Plan Template

This template can be used by school resilience planners as the basis of their emergency response plans. It is not an exhaustive list and planners should add / remove detail as appropriate to their situation.

Emergency Response Plan for

.................................School

School Address:

Emergency Plan Author:
Name:

Appointment:

Critical School Contact Information (name and 24 / 7 contact):
Head Teacher:

Deputy Head teacher:

Key-holder(s):

Emergency point of contact:

Reception:

Other:

Version Control:
Version Number:

Date:

A1. Aim of the Emergency Response Plan

The aim of the emergency plan is to describe how the school will respond to an emergency in order to save lives and prevent further injury to the school community in the event of a potential or actual life-threatening emergency.

A2. Objectives of the Emergency Response Plan

The objectives of the school emergency response plan are:

- To describe the locality in general, especially with regards to key locations.
- To describe the school geography in detail, especially with regards to key locations.
- To identify key responders (and deputies) including the Incident Management Team.
- To identify possible hazards and identify appropriate strategies for managing the response.
- To identify potential triggers for plan activation.
- To identify the Immediate Actions of the responders and school community.
- To identify how the Incident Management Team will communicate with the extended school community.
- To identify key locations relevant to the implementation of the plan.
- To identify critical contact information required in the response.
- To identify a training and exercising schedule.
- To identify a plan audit and review process.

A.3 Key Local Institutions

The following are the addresses of important local institutions in the school neighbourhood:

- **Police Station:**

- **Fire and Rescue Station:**

- **Ambulance Service:**

- **Hospital (with Accident and Emergency):**

- **GP surgery:**

- **Primary Care Trust:**

- **Local Authority:**

- **Other schools:**

- **Other:**

A.4 Key Locations

The following are key locations to the school plan:

- **Primary IMT Location – Emergency Operations Centre (EOC):**

- **Secondary IMT Location (EOC):**

- **Assembly area:**

- **Alternate Assembly area:**

- **Primary Place of Safety:**

- **Secondary Place of Safety:**

- **Route to Primary Place of Safety:**

- **Route to Secondary Place of Safety:**

- **Parent Reception Areas:**

- **Potential shelters within school:**

- **Designated shelter for outside areas:**

- **"Quiet" room for Recovery purposes:**

- **Media information point:**

- **Media centre:**

A.5 Incident Management Team

The following are members of the Incident Management Team:

- **Incident Manager:**

- **Deputy Incident Manager:**

- **Media Liaison Officer:**

- **Media Liaison Assistant:**

- **Parent Liaison Officer:**

- **Parent Liaison Assistant:**

- **Logistics Coordinator:**

- **Governing Body Representative:**

- **Emergency Point of Contact:**

The role of the Incident Management Team in the response is to ensure the following:

- Ongoing assessment of the situation and its implications.
- Ensuring the well-being of those at the scene.
- Liaising with the emergency services.
- Establishing reliable communications with staff / emergency services at the scene.
- Communicating with the school community.
- To account for all members of the school community.
- Ensuring the well-being of the entire school community.
- Informing the Local Authority and ongoing liaison.
- Informing the parents of the injured and assisting them as required.
- Informing all parents of the situation.

- Working with the Police with regards to informing parents / family of the deceased (if any).
- Managing media requests.

The Incident Management Team (IMT) generic roles and responsibility are:

Incident Manager:
- Activates the alarm (when not already activated).
- Leads the response to the incident.
- Makes unilateral decisions if the situation requires.
- Not the designated Media liaison officer, although can make statements.

Deputy Incident Manager
- Deputises for the Incident Manager in absence.
- Coordinates with teachers in the school not in the IMT (e.g. accounting for staff).

Parent Liaison team:
- Responsible for coordination of information to parents.
- Coordinates information requests from parents.
- Acts as a point of contact for parents.
- May require a team to support telephones.

Media Liaison team:
- Responsible for the preparation of the media information packs.
- Point of contact for the Media during the response.
- Provide constant flow of information to the Media.
- Liaise with Local Authority Communications Officer(s) / Press Relations Officer(s).

Logistics Coordinator:
- Coordinates logistic / facilities / security related tasks.
- Usually Facilities Manager.

Administration
- Keep minutes of IMT meetings.
- Log activities and decisions.
- Answering telephone calls.

- "Runner" for passing messages.

Representative of Governing Body
- Often Head Governor.
- Provide the strategic overview of the response from the school perspective.
- Provide a "talking head" for the Media.
- Provides support to the IMT / Incident Manager.

A.6 Plan Activation

Criteria for activating the plan:
The plan will be activated under the following circumstances:

- On activation of the fire alarm.
- On receipt of a telephone call by the emergency point of contact.
- On being informed of a bomb threat.
- On being informed of an external threat (toxic plume; criminal etc).
- On being informed of an intruder within the school.
- On being informed of a sudden illness in the school.
- On receipt of information that the head teacher considers requires the plan to be activated.

Authority for activating the plan:
The plan will be activated by the Head Teacher or his deputy who will take on the role of Incident Manager. By default, any individual who activates the fire alarm will also activate the plan.

School Alert Mechanisms:
The School Emergency Plan will generally be activated by one of two alarms. The alarms should be activated as described below:

Fire Alarm:
- Fires.
- Explosions.
- Immediate evacuation.

Lockdown (intermittently sounding) Alarm:
- Bomb threat.

- Intruder on site.
- Sheltering (general, quarantine).
- Threat outside the school.
- Accidental death or serious injury on school premises.

The following incident types will not require an immediate activation by alarm, but would still require the emergency plan to be activated:

- Incident on school trip.
- Death or injury outside the school premises, outside school hours.

A.7 Emergency Response – Immediate Actions:

Overview

The over-riding aim of the plan is to save life and / or prevent further injury. To that end, the initial response at the scene of the incident – whether at the school or away from it - is to ensure that professional assistance is on the way – summoning the Emergency Services is critical.

Information must be passed to the Emergency Point of Contact who is able to initiate the activation of the plan, by informing the Incident Manager. The Incident Manager will make the first assessment while the Emergency Point of Contact warns and informs the remainder of the Incident Management Team.

The Incident Manager will act on the initial assessment appropriately to the hazard / threat. In essence, advice given will be to evacuate or shelter (initially by lockdown). For an off-site emergency, the Incident Management Team will manage the incident from the school.

The Incident Management Team will meet at a pre-agreed location, make further assessments and manage the response to the remainder of the incident, liaising as appropriate with the Emergency Services and Local Authority.

The Media may be involved, in which case they need to be managed. There may be a requirement to deploy teachers to hospitals.

The passage of accurate and timely information is critical at all times.

Responses to Specific Hazards / Threats
The following list outlines possible hazards or threats and the identified contingency strategies to mitigate that hazard or threat.

School trip (away from the school premises):
- IMT to manage the incident from EOC.
- Close liaison with staff or emergency services at the scene.

Death or injury outside of school hours (away from school premises):
- IMT to manage the incident from EOC.
- Close liaison with emergency services, local authority and parents.

Accidental death or injury on school site:
- IMT to manage the incident from EOC.
- Close liaison with staff or emergency services at the scene.
- Temporary lockdown to establish control of situation.
- Business continuity plan

Violent intruder on school site; incident over:
- IMT to manage the incident from EOC.
- Close liaison with staff or emergency services at the scene.
- Temporary lockdown to establish control of situation.
- Be prepared to shelter or evacuate further.

Violent intruder on school site; incident ongoing:
- IMT to manage the incident from EOC – if possible.
- Close liaison with staff or emergency services at the scene.
- Temporary lockdown to establish control of situation.
- Be prepared to evacuate to assembly point / alternate assembly point or place of safety - if possible.

External threat (criminal) outside school perimeter:
- IMT to manage the incident from EOC.
- Close liaison with staff or emergency services at the scene.
- Temporary lockdown to establish control of situation.
- Business continuity plan

External hazard (toxic plume / smoke etc) outside school perimeter:
- IMT to manage the incident from EOC.
- Close liaison with staff or emergency services at the scene.
- Temporary lockdown to establish control of situation.
- Shelter in classrooms / identified safe location within the school.

Sudden illness on school premises:
- IMT to manage the incident from EOC.
- Isolation and segregation at the scene.
- Close liaison with staff or emergency services at the scene.
- Temporary lockdown to establish control of situation.
- Business continuity plan

Fire / explosion:
- Evacuate to assembly area.
- Close liaison with emergency services at the school.
- IMT to manage the situation from external place of safety.
- Onward evacuation to place of safety.
- Business continuity / collection of children.

Bomb threat:
- IMT to manage the incident initially from EOC.
- Close liaison with emergency services to establish authenticity.
- Temporary lockdown to establish control of situation.
- Controlled evacuation to assembly area (or alternate assembly area) if threat is confirmed.
- Onward evacuation to place of safety.
- Business continuity / collection of children.

A.8 Immediate Actions - Staff Member at scene of the incident

The priority of the staff member at the scene – whether at the school or away from the school - is to save life and prevent further injury. In the event of an emergency / incident, the staff member at the scene should act as follows:

Initial Response at scene:
- Save life, if possible.
- Summon the appropriate emergency service(s). Inform them of:

- o Which emergency service you require – or all three.
- o Where you are.
- o Who are you – include numbers of children and adults.
- o What has happened and when.
- o What you are now doing.
- o Your contact details.
- Protect the lives of remaining students – possibly by moving them to a place of safety.
- Alert the IMT through the emergency point of contact (*see box below for information required by the IMT*).
- Brief the emergency services on numbers of children / details of school.
- If any members of the school community have been taken to hospital, note which students and which hospital (liaise with the Ambulance service representative at the scene).
- Ensure communications available to continue to report to the IMT.
- Manage the incident as best as possible.
- Continue to provide regular updates to the emergency point of contact / IMT.
- Maintain a log of actions.

Information to be provided to the Emergency Point of Contact from the scene of the incident:

- Who you are and confirm contact details.
- Confirm that the emergency services have been summoned and whether they are on scene.
- Confirm whether or not there is an ongoing threat / hazard to the school community.
- What has happened, when and where?
- Who is involved from the school community and what is their condition?
- Has everyone been accounted for? Where is everyone?
- What is now happening?
- Have any of the school community been taken to hospital? Which hospital?
- Are there any specific requirements from the scene?
- Any other information that the trip / activity leader believes appropriate.

A.9 Immediate Actions - Emergency Point of Contact

On receipt of the notification of an emergency (excluding a fire drill), the emergency point of contact will need to carry out a number of tasks to ensure that the emergency procedures are followed.

The emergency point of contact will:

- Log all information.
- Confirm the emergency services have been summoned.
- Call emergency services if not yet done.
- Inform Incident Manager of the situation.
- Undertake tasks as instructed by the IMT.
- Inform remainder of the IMT.
- Inform the Local Authority emergency number.
- Call back staff member at scene for updates.

On hearing the fire alarm, the emergency point of contact will carry out the following actions:

- Evacuate in accordance with the fire drill, taking the daily register.
- Ensure that the emergency services have been summoned.
- Call emergency services if not yet done.
- Join IMT at the Assembly Area.
- Inform the Local Authority emergency number.
- Undertake tasks as instructed by the IMT.

A.10 Immediate Actions - Incident Manager

On hearing the fire alarm, the Incident Manager will act in accordance with the fire drill, meeting the IMT at the Assembly Area. Key tasks include:

- Start log.
- Receiving reports from staff and accounting for all students.
- Ensure that the Fire & Rescue Service are met and have all available information.
- Decide on further actions, such as evacuation to place of safety.
- If appropriate, ensure that parents are informed of the situation

through the parent liaison officer.
- If appropriate, ensure that the Media are informed of the situation through the Media liaison officer.
- Ensure that the Local Authority is informed.

On being informed of an incident by the emergency point of contact or other source, the Incident Manager will need to make an assessment of the situation and make several decisions.

Initial impact assessment:

- Confirm the aim - to save life and prevent further injury.
- What is the hazard?
- Where is the hazard?
- Where is the "scene"?
- Where are the school community? Consider those at the scene and the remainder of the school community.
- What are the possible consequences of the hazard to the school community?
- What is the future threat to the school community and how can this be mitigated?

Decide:

- The advice to give to those at the scene in order to save life and protect against further injury.
- How best to protect the remainder of the school community:
    - o   Evacuate.
    - o   Shelter – lockdown / refuge / quarantine.
- Whether there is a need to alert the remainder of the school and if so, how best could this be done and what message should be provided.
- Where to convene the IMT – primary or secondary location.
- Who is to meet the Emergency Services to escort them to the scene.
- Who will liaise with the Emergency Services.
- Confirm release of parents' holding statement.
- Confirm release of Media holding statement.

The subsequent role of the Incident Manager is as follows:

- To lead the response to the emergency.
- Account for all members of the school community, identifying those who are not directly involved, the involved but uninjured, the injured and the deceased.
- Access student emergency contact details as required.
- To coordinate the activities of the IMT.
- To confirm a media strategy with the Media Liaison officer.
- Maintain contact with the scene.
- To be available to act as a spokesperson at certain times.
- Decide who should attend the hospital(s) on behalf of the school.
- Liaise with and request assistance from the local authority as required.

A.11 Immediate Actions - Deputy Incident Manager

The Deputy Incident Manager has a number of specific tasks (see below). She / he is also the individual who will stand in for the Incident Manager in his / her absence. In such cases, the tasks of the Deputy Incident Manager must be assigned to another individual.

On hearing the fire alarm, the Deputy Incident Manager will act in accordance with the fire drill, meeting the IMT at the Assembly Area.

On hearing the intermittent alarm, the Deputy Incident Manager will ensure that their students are supervised and accounted for and will then make their way to the EOC.

Key tasks include:

- Start log.
- Liaise with the staff member at the scene.
- Identify which members of the school community have been affected and to what extent (fatalities, injured, involved but uninjured, not involved). (Inform Parent Liaison Officer).
- Liaise with police regarding the emergency contact information of those children who have been killed (inform Parent Liaison Officer).
- Provide support to the Incident Manager and stand in for that

individual in the event of his / her absence.
- Manage the passage of information to the remainder of the school community.
- Ensure business continuity for the remainder of the school not directly affected by the incident.

A.12 Immediate Actions - Media Liaison Team

Media Liaison Officer
The Media Liaison Officer is the focal point for all media activity at the school.

On hearing the fire alarm, the Media Liaison Officer will act in accordance with the fire drill, meeting the IMT at the Assembly Area.

On hearing the intermittent alarm, the Media Liaison Officer will ensure that their students are supervised and accounted for and will then make their way to the EOC.

Specific tasks are to:

- Start log.
- Provide an initial holding statement to the media .
- Provide the initial point of contact for all media requests.
- Provide the Media with the Media information packs.
- Maintain regular contact with the media, providing appropriate information as required.
- Liaise with the local authority communications team in order to identify an appropriate strategy.
- Confirm strategy with the Incident Manager.
- To be the school spokesperson.
- To identify a suitable location for the media information point.
- To work with the local authority communications team to identify a suitable media centre.
- Brief the Incident Manager at regular intervals on the media picture.

Media Assistant
The media assistant will support the media liaison officer as follows:

On hearing the fire alarm, the media assistant will act in accordance with the fire drill, meeting the IMT at the Assembly Area.

On hearing the intermittent alarm, the media assistant will ensure that their students are supervised and accounted for and will then make their way to the EOC. Further tasks include:

- Start log
- Answer phone requests for information, providing verbal statements as agreed with the Media Liaison Officer.
- Monitor the local and national radio / TV news bulletins and Internet and brief Media Liaison Officer
- To respond to email / fax request for information.
- To liaise with the local authority communications team as appropriate.
- Update website to ensure accurate information available to parents.

A.13 Immediate Actions - Parent Liaison Team

The Parent Liaison Officer and Assistant are to act as the focal point for parents at the school.

On hearing the fire alarm, the parent liaison team will act in accordance with the fire drill, meeting the IMT at the Assembly Area.

On hearing the intermittent alarm, the parent liaison team will ensure that their students are supervised and accounted for and will then make their way to the EOC.

Specific tasks of the parent liaison team are:

- Start log.
- Issue an initial message to all parents (see below).
- Locate all emergency contact information for those children affected by the incident.
- Liaise with Deputy Incident Manager regarding status of children.
- Contact parents of injured children and inform them of location of hospital.
- Ensure emergency services have emergency contact information for parents of deceased children.

- Liaise with Media Liaison Officer for information updates to be sent to local radio.
- Provide information updates to media assistant for publication on web site.

A.14 Immediate Actions - Logistics Coordinator

The Logistics Coordinator is responsible for organising all logistical matters for the

On hearing the fire alarm, the media assistant will act in accordance with the fire drill, meeting the IMT at the Assembly Area.

On hearing the intermittent alarm, the media assistant will ensure that their students are supervised and accounted for and will then make their way to the EOC.

Specific tasks may include:

- Start log.
- Provision of suitable accommodation for sheltering.
- Provision of transportation for parents to hospital(s).

A.15 Immediate Actions - School Community

On hearing the fire alarm.

The school community not involved in the emergency / incident should act in accordance with the fire drill.

- Evacuate by the nearest exit to the assembly area.
- Members of the IMT should congregate around the Incident Manager once own students are safe and supervised by other staff members.

On hearing the intermittent alarm.

Those members of the school community not involved in the emergency / incident should carry out the following actions:

- Staff members to account for all students in their care.

- Staff members looking after students should close and lock the doors to their classrooms.
- Staff members to turn on their mobile phones and wait for instructions from the Incident Management Team.
- Staff members on the Incident Management Team should arrange for their students to be supervised, then make their way to the IMT EOC.
- All students should remain in their current location, or (where possible and viable), return immediately to their classrooms.
- *Variations, based on student age group, size of school, layout of school etc.*

A.16 Media Plan

The Media plan is put into practice by the Media Liaison Team and covers the following:

- Staff / students at scene not to make comment to Media.
- Identify holding area for Media outside school.
- Release of media pack to Media.
- Release holding statement.
- Liaise with Local Authority and emergency services communications teams.
- Preparation of ongoing media statements.
- Update school website with information.
- Identify location for press conference.
- "Talking head" at press conference.
- Anticipate Media awaiting return of students.

The initial holding statement for the Media is:

- The fact that there has been an incident involving trip / class / entire school.
- The school is liaising with the emergency services to account for the students and staff.
- The school has activated its emergency plan.
- The school will contact the parents and media as soon as it has any more information.
- Parents should stay next to the phone so that they can be contacted as soon as more information is known.

A.17 Parent Liaison Plan

The parent liaison plan is put into practice by the Parent Liaison Team and covers the following:

- Provision of generic information message to local radio.
  - o Holding statement.
  - o Stay contactable.
  - o Parents to stay at home until situation clarified.
- Parents of injured and evacuated informed and directed to appropriate hospital(s).
- Be prepared to provide reception facilities for parents of uninjured / involved.
- Ongoing provision of information.
- Update school internet site –parents' site.
- Bereaved parents to be informed by police.
- Provision of information letter.
- Parents of uninjured / uninvolved to be informed of collection procedures.

The initial message to parents will include:

- The fact that there has been an incident involving trip / class / entire school.
- The school is liaising with the emergency services to account for the students and staff.
- The school has activated its emergency plan.
- The school will contact parents as soon as they have any more information.
- Parents should stay next to the phone so that they can be contacted as soon as more information is known.
- More information will be made available either directly or on the local radio station (provide station name and frequency).

A.18 Medical

Infectious disease:

In the event of a number of members of the school community becoming ill at the same time, the following should happen:

- Summon the ambulance service.
- Isolate the student group.

- Segregate those who are symptomatic and those who are not (preferably in separate rooms).
- Inform the emergency point of contact.
- Treat the symptoms of those who are ill.
- Monitor the non-symptomatic group, moving any newly symptomatic students to the appropriate group.

Casualties:
In the event of casualties, the following should happen:

- Provide initial first aid.
- Ambulance service response.
- Liaison with Ambulance Service.
- Accounting for injured.
- Communicating with IMT and keeping them informed.
- Informing parents.
- Parents to hospital(s).
- Member of staff / Local Authority to hospital(s).

Fatalities:
In the event of an incident involving fatalities, the following should be considered:

- Accounting for who is deceased.
- Emergency service response.
- Emergency Contact information to police.
- Liaison of IMT with police and FLOs.
- Informing local authority (social care).
- Communicating with bereaved.
- Communicating with all parents.

A.19 Recovery Plan

Following an emergency, the school will move into a period of recovery led by the IMT. The following issues should be considered:

Structural Issues:
- Forensic examination.
- Partial / full closure.
- Decontamination / sanitisation.
- Reconstruction.

- Alternative locations.
- School reopening.

Practical Issues:
- Caring for the victims.
- Practical assistance to students / parents (financial, benefits etc).
- Business continuity management for remainder of school.

Psychological issues
- Caring for the victims.
- Managing impact on the school community.
- Memorials.
- Availability of educational psychologists.
- Indirect victims – consider siblings / friends / classmates / team-mates of deceased / injured etc.
- Anniversaries.

A.20 Communications

Emergency Operations Centre (EOC)

The EOC has the following communications facilities:

- Landline (6 lines).
- Mobile phones (with staff).
- Email.
- Internet and Intranet publishing capability.

Communications during an emergency:

The following are the principal mechanisms for communicating in an emergency:

- Fire alarm and lockdown alarm to signal evacuation and lockdown respectively.
- Landline / mobile communications with emergency services and external organisations.
- Mobile phone to staff for one-to-one communication.
- Mobile phone texting for one-to-many communication.
- Email to staff computers during lockdown.

A.21 Hierarchy of control and coordination

In the event of the Incident Manager not being available, the deputy incident manager will step in.

The deputy incident manager will be replaced by *(name)*.

In the event of the Deputy Incident Manager not being available as well, the *(appointment)* will step in.

In such circumstances, the replacement for the Incident Manager will be *(name)* and the replacement for the deputy incident manager will be *(name)*.

A.22 Appendices

Appendices can be added to the plan to enhance the detail of the response. Examples include:

- General map of area

- Detailed map of school

- Emergency point of contact form

- Media pack – contents and location

- "Emergency off-site pack" – contents and location

- Initial Media holding statement

- Initial information statement for parents

- Children collection plan – own school

- Children collection plan – place of safety

- Bomb threat procedures

- Training, exercising, audit and review

- Contact Information

Annex B - School Business Continuity Management Programme Template

This template programme can be used by school resilience planners as the basis of their business continuity management programme and subsequent plan.

It is not exhaustive and planners should add / remove detail as appropriate to the situation.

Note that this is the Programme template – from which the planner will derive the information required to undertake the planning process itself.

B.1 Introduction

The following is a possible template for a school's Business Continuity Management Programme. The completion of a BCM Programme is the first step – this provides the framework for the business continuity planning process. The second step is the implementation of the BCM Programme, the outcome of which is the full Business Continuity Plan. There would then need to be a continuous process of training, exercising, review and maintenance of both the BCP and the Programme to ensure that both documents remain valid, viable and focussed on the school management's critical areas.

B.2 BCM Policy

The BCM Policy will provide the strategic guidance for the BCM Programme and show a statement of intent by the employer, Governors and school management.

The policy may include:

- Scope of policy.
- Legislative background.
- Outcomes.
- Standards to be achieved.
- Outline contents of the BCM Programme, to include specifically:
    - o Specific critical activities for which a BCM plan must be considered, for example:
        - ☐ Emergency response capability.
    - o Criteria for identifying critical activities for which a BCM plan must be considered, to include:
        - ☐ Statutory duties.
        - ☐ Duty of Care / health and safety.
- Planning levels – for example, all departments to undertake BCM under the overview of the School BCM lead.
- Requirement that all contracts include the requirement for verified and effective BCM plans.
- Requirements for training, exercising and plan validation.
- Details of audit and review.

Note that, depending on the size of the school, BCM planning may be undertaken at Departmental level initially – possibly by Heads of Department with assistance from the resilience planner - and then the outputs pulled together by the resilience planner to provide a single coordinated plan.

B.3 BCM Programme

The BCM Programme will provide the strategic framework for the BCM process. Initially it will identify the foundation of the BCM process, including:

Identifying roles & responsibilities:
- Employer representative: *(Local Authority)*.
- Programme Management: *(Head Teacher & Head Governor)*.
- BCM planner: *(School emergency planner)*. *Responsible for school level plan and coordinating departmental plans.*
- Departmental planners (if required).

Identifying the output of the overall process:
- BCM Policy.
- BCM Programme – (this document, based on the BS-25999 six phase approach).
- Business Continuity Plan.

B.4 Understanding the Organisation

Following this phase, the BCM Programme will need to identify the criteria for the introspective analysis of the school itself – described as "Understanding the Organisation" in the BS:25999 standard.

The outcome of this phase is to identify the Mission Critical Activities (MCA) of the school. It will assess the resources required to continue the activity. It will identify any vulnerabilities in the resources. It will consider each MCA in light of a number of risk consequences and will identify a number of Business Continuity operational strategies that can either be implemented immediately to prevent an incident occurring or to mitigate the impact of an incident as part of the BCP response. It is a three phase exercise and the first stage is the Business Impact Analysis (BIA).

B.5 Business Impact Analysis (BIA)

The first stage of this is to identify all activities undertaken by the school. Once this is completed the activities will be measures against the critical activity criteria (below) to identify what are critical activities.

The following information should be identified in the BCM Programme:

- Criteria for identifying critical activities for which a BCM plan must be considered:
    - o Where the loss of the activity will result in a hazard to life and limb.
    - o Where the loss of the activity will result in a failure to provide a statutory duty.
    - o Where the loss of the activity will result in severe reputational damage to the employer or the school.
    - o Where the loss of the activity will result in a financial loss to the employer or school.
    - o Where an activity is designated as a critical activity for the employer or another school.

Having identified the critical activities it is necessary to understand how quickly they need to be restored to the basic level and for how long the school can refrain from undertaking the activities.

- Recovery timeframes – Recovery Time Objective (RTO) and Maximum Tolerable Period of Disruption (MTPD):
    - o Immediate.
    - o Between 1 – 2 hours.
    - o Within 24 hours.
    - o Within a week.
    - o Between 1 week and 1 month.
    - o Over 1 month.

For the same critical activities, the planner need to know what would be the impact if the activity was not being undertaken.

- Definition of possible impacts (NB – also note those that may increase impact if not treated over a period of time):

- o Intolerable.
- o High.
- o Medium.
- o Low.
- o Negligible.

Understanding the criticality, the timeframes and impact of loss, it is possible to assess those critical activities which are Mission Critical Activities.

- Criteria for identification of Mission Critical Activities:
    - o Any critical activity with an intolerable impact.
    - o Any activity with an immediate, 1-2 hours or under 1 day RTO.
    - o Any activity with a high impact and an RTO of less than one week.
    - o Any activity with a high impact and an MTPD of less than one month.

These are the Mission Critical Activities and will be the focus of subsequent analysis and planning.

B.6 Resource Assessment

A resource assessment should be undertaken for each Mission Critical Activity to understand what resources would be required to continue the MCA at both its most basic and normal levels. Resources should be considered under the following headings:

- People.
- Facilities.
- Equipment.
- Information Technology.
- Communications.
- Information.
- Critical interdependencies.
- Other.

Any vulnerabilities should be noted and preventative action should be noted and where possible implemented. Where Business Continuity operational strategies to mitigate the impact of an incident are identified these should be noted for inclusion in the BCP.

B.7 Risk Review

The BCM Programme requires that the Mission Critical Activities are assessed against the following risks in order to identify what would be the impact and to identify appropriate strategies to mitigate the consequences.

The risk review contingency planning assumptions are as follows:

- Large scale temporary absence of staff – up to 35% over a 2-3 week period.
- Permanent or long-term loss of staff – through death / serious injury.
- Denial of site or geographical area:
- Loss of mains electricity:
- Disruption to transport:
- Loss of mains water and sewerage:
- Loss of availability of oil and fuel – disruption for up to 10 days.
- Loss of gas - short term losses to localities; restored within days. (May also cause 3 hour electricity power rotations).
- Loss of electronic communications.
- Loss of IT

Where weaknesses or vulnerabilities are identified, the planner should identify operational strategies that will mitigate these. Along with those from the resource assessment, these operational strategies will form the basis of the final BCP.

B.8 Determining BCM strategies

For the remaining mission critical activities, the BCM Programme Management will consider the appropriate risk treatment strategy to be adopted. These can be:

- **Tolerate.** Accept the critical activity as it stands with no further planning required.
- **Transfer.** Transfer the risk to another school; some risks may

be transferred by insurance.

- **Terminate.** The risk is so great and the possible strategies to mitigate the risk so costly in time or resources, that the critical activity should be stopped.
- **Treat.** Create business continuity plans for these critical activities.

B.9 Developing a Business Continuity Plan

Effective BCPs need to be prepared in order to ensure the continuity of Mission Critical Activities in accordance with the scale and timeframe identified in the earlier phases of the Programme.

BCPs for Departments with Mission Critical Activities will include:

- An overall point of contact for the Service.

- An incident management structure in the event of an internal disruption.

- An activation mechanism for the BCP.

- Immediate response tasks.

- Roles and responsibilities.

- Deputies for specific roles.

- Locations from where tasks will be conducted.

- Alternate locations from where tasks will be conducted if the primary location is unavailable.

- The resources required for the tasks, where they are located and from where further resources can be sourced.

- Specific contingency strategies for specific issues – as identified in the risk review.

- Inter-dependencies with other services and organisations and how these will be operated during the response.

- A list of non-Mission Critical Activities in priority order for recovery, based on BIA, RO and MTPD.

- A list of all other critical activities, prioritised by Recovery Time Objective (RTO).

- All key contacts.

- Confirm that all managers can contact their staff through team-held contact information.

Where a Department has no Mission Critical Activities, the following information will be required in their Business Continuity Plan:

- A Service / Team point of contact.

- An incident management structure.

- The mechanism for briefing Strategic Director / Head of Service.

- Deputies for specific roles.

- An information cascade systems for the activation of the Service plan and ongoing passage of information.

- Immediate tasks for the Service / Teams.

- Alternative locations from where to undertake work if possible.

- Identify for how long the Services' / Teams' activities can be non-operational.

- A list of all critical activities, prioritised by Recovery Time.

- Contact Information.

B.10 Next stages

The BCM Programme should identify the training, exercising, review and maintenance process. It should also include how BCM should be embedded in the culture of the organisation.

Annex C - Sample School Exercises

The following two exercise scenarios may be used as the basis of a tabletop exercise for a school IMT or as an example of how such exercises may be framed.

Introduction

The following are examples of some scenarios and related questions that could be used in a basic tabletop exercise. Both scenario and questions can be enhanced to make them more appropriate for the school.

Scenario 1 – school trip

Inject 1:
Information to the IMT:
- Class / Year (name) is travelling to see a museum in (name). There are 45 children on the bus, with teacher supervision.

Questions / considerations for the IMT:
- What preparations would need to be made prior to the trip?
- Who makes them?

Inject 2:
Information to the IMT:
- The school's emergency contact receives a call from the teacher in charge. There has just been an accident on the road and their bus was involved.
- They've called the emergency services.
- Some children are hurt.

Questions / considerations for the IMT:
- What does the school's emergency contact do?
- What does the Incident Manager do?
- What is your assessment of the situation?

Inject 3:
Information to the IMT:
- It is 10 minutes later. The teacher at the scene has called back.
- The emergency services have arrived on the scene.
- She has taken the uninjured and slightly children to a safe location by the side of the road.
- Two children have been taken to hospital.
- One child is missing but the emergency services are still searching the wreckage of the bus.

- One of the children was seen talking on his mobile phone.

Questions / considerations for the IMT:
- What is the latest assessment of the situation?
- What are your main concerns?
- What should the Incident Management Team do?

Inject 4:
Information to the IMT:
- It is 5 minutes later.
- A parent rings into the school asking questions about whether their child is ok. They've heard about the accident. Within minutes 2 more ring in.
- The local radio station also calls.

Questions / considerations for the IMT:
- What is your assessment of the situation?
- What do you tell the parents?
- What do you tell the media?
- What further action should you take with regards to parents and media?
- What else will you do?

Inject 5:
Information to the IMT:
- The teacher at the scene calls back. The missing child has been found – she had wandered off from the area.
- The ambulance service have confirmed the two injured children have broken bones, but the injuries are not life threatening.

Questions / considerations for the IMT:
- What is your assessment of the situation?
- What do you do now?

Scenario 2 – fire in the vicinity of the school

Inject 1:
Information to the IMT:
- It is 10.45 am. A teacher notices a fire in a nearby industrial unit. Fire-fighters are dealing with it and there is no threat to the school from fire, however there is a lot of smoke.
- A fire-fighter comes over to the school and informs the reception of the fire and that the school should shelter.

Questions / considerations for the IMT:
- What is your assessment of the situation?
- What does the reception do?
- What does the Incident Manager do?
- What does the Incident Management Team do?

Inject 2:
Information to the IMT:
- A parent rings in asking about the smoke they can see from the area.
- A local newspaper journalist is taking photographs.

Questions / considerations for the IMT:
- What is your assessment and what do you do?

Inject 3:
Information to the IMT:
- The fire-fighter returns to reception and explains that they have located an acetylene cylinder in the fire and they must put in a 200 metre cordon for 24 hours.
- The school is within 200 metres of the fire and therefore they must evacuate as quickly as possible.
- However, the primary assembly area is between the fire and the school.

Questions / considerations for the IMT:
- What is the latest assessment of the situation?
- What are your main concerns?
- What should the Incident Management Team do?
- How do you activate the evacuation?
- Where do you go?

Inject 4:
Information to the IMT:
- You go to the secondary assembly area and then your buddy school.
- All children have been accounted for.
- There is no space to continue classes, but the children are safe.

Questions / considerations for the IMT:
- What is your assessment of the situation?
- What do you tell the parents and media?
- What else will you do?

Inject 5:
Information to the IMT:
- You decide to close the school for the day.
- Most children can be collected, however there are a number whose parents are working and who have no one to collect them or look after them until the end of the normal school day.

Questions / considerations for the IMT:
- How do you organise the collection of children?
- How do you account for the children?
- What do you tell the parents?
- What do you do with the remaining children?

BIBLIOGRAPHY

Bradford J (2000). *From Lyme Bay to Licensing* [online]. Adventure Activities Licensing Authority. www.aala.org/lymebay01.html. [23 September, 2004].

British Red Cross (1999). *Disaster Appeal Scheme (UK).* London. British Red Cross Society.

British Standards Institution (2006). *BS25999-1:2006.* British Standards Institution.

Brock S.E. Sandoval J. and Lewis S. (2001). *Preparing for Crises in the Schools. A Manual for Building School Crisis Response Teams.* 2nd edition. United States of America. John Wiley & Sons, Inc.

Campion M. (1998). *Jupiter's Children.* Liverpool. Liverpool University Press.

Croner's (1993). *The Teacher's Legal Guide.* Kingston upon Thames. Croner Publications Ltd.

Cullen, The Rt. Hon. Lord W D (1996). *Public Inquiry Into The Shootings At Dunblane Primary School On 13 March 1996.* The Scottish Office.

Davies E. (1967). Report of the Tribunal Appointed to Inquire into the Disaster at Aberfan on October 21st

Edwards G (1998). Dunblane. An emergency planning unit's response. *Emergencies Involving Children.* Warwickshire Emergency Planning Unit. 15th October 1998.

Fein A.H. (2003). *There and Back Again. School Shootings as Experienced by School Leaders.* USA. Scarecrow Press, Inc.

Fyfe A A J (2005). *A Critical Review of the Emergency Response to School Incidents by Schools and Local Education Authorities.* University of Hertfordshire, United Kingdom.

Hodgkinson P E and Stewart M (2001). *Coping with Catastrophe. A Handbook of Post-Disaster Psychological Aftercare.* 2nd Edition. Hove, UK. Brunner-Routledge.

Jefferson County Sheriff's Office, Colorado (2009). *Primary Time Line for April 20, 1999* [online] http://jefferson.lib.co.us/columbine-cd/Columbine%20REPORT/Pages/TOC.htm [July 2009]

Jenkin S and Jenkinson P (1995). *The Lyme Bay Canoeing Tragedy: 22nd March 1993.* Devon County Council.

Johnes M and McLean I (2000). *Aberfan. Government and Disasters.* Cardiff

Kendall P (2004). *Collenswood School, Stevenage Incident. Thursday 9th September 2004. Draft Multi-Agency Debrief Report.* Hertfordshire Emergency Services Major Incident Committee (HESMIC CBRN Working Group).

Kibble D G (1999). A survey of LEA guidance and support for the management of crises in schools. *School Leadership & Management.* **19.** 3. 373

Motomura N (2002). School crisis intervention in the Ikeda incident: Organisation and activity of the mental support team. Psychiatry and Clinical Neurosciences (2003) **57**, 239-240.

National Steering Committee for Warning and Informing the Public (2004). *Go In, Stay In, Tune In* [online]. www.nscwip.info/goinstayintunein.htm [13th January 2005]

National Union of Teachers. (2003). *Emergency procedures in Schools: NUT Health and Safety Briefing.* [online]. www.teachers.

org.uk/resources/pdf/emergency-procedures.pdf   [21st December 2004].

North, Dr. M. (2000). *Dunblane: Never Forget.* Great Britain. Mainstream Publishing Company (Edinburgh) Ltd.

Rabjohn, A (2004). No Playtime Today. *When Disaster Strikes In Education.* Bracknell. 20th May 2004.

Rath T (1989). Calthorp Park School Fleet: Coach Accident 29th June 1989. Report of the County Education Officer. [online] www.hants.gov.uk/scrmxn/c2404.html [14th December 2004]

Shears J. (1995) Managing Tragedy in a Secondary School In Smith S.C. and Pennells M. (eds). *Interventions With Bereaved Children.* London, UK. Jessica Kingsley Publishers. 241-253.

Stirling Council (1999). *Dunblane: A Place Of Learning.*

Stirling Council (1999). *Should Crisis Call...Crisis Management In Schools: Effective Preparation And Response.*

United Kingdom. Cabinet Office (2004). *Civil Contingencies Act 2004.* London. HMSO.

United Kingdom. Cabinet Office (2005). *Emergency Preparedness.* HM Government.

United Kingdom. Cabinet Office (2009). 2nd edition. *Emergency Response and Recovery.* HM Government.

United Kingdom. The Scottish Office (1996) *The Public Inquiry Into The Shootings At Dunblane Primary School On 13 March 1996: The Government Response.* Edinburgh. Stationery Office.

United States of America, State of Alaska (1999). School Crisis Response Planning Act. [online] SB125. www.securitymanagement.com/library/SB125.html [27th January 2005]

Wanko M A. (2001). *Safe Schools. Crisis Prevention and Response.* Maryland USA. Scarecrow Press, Inc.

Yule W and Gold A (1993). *Wise Before The Event.* London. Calouste Gulbenkian Foundation.

About The Author

The author is the Resilience Manager in a top tier local authority in the UK, with responsibilities for emergency management and business continuity management. This includes advising the Schools Service and individual schools within the county.

He has an MSc in Emergency Planning and Disaster Management, during the completion of which he undertook a project on school emergency planning, and he is a member of the Emergency Planning Society. He has been involved in the response to a number of emergencies, including several school incidents. He has a Diploma in Business Continuity Management and is a member of the Business Continuity Institute. He is also a member of the International Association of Emergency Management.

Before joining the Local Authority, he worked for four years in Bosnia with the Organisation for Security and Cooperation in Europe (OSCE). There he was responsible for the training of international election supervisors and then the planning and conduct of elections in eight municipalities. His last role was as a Deputy Director for one of the four Regional Centres. Prior to his time with the OSCE he served as an officer in the British Army, serving on operations in Belize and Bosnia.

Breinigsville, PA USA
23 February 2010
233081BV00002B/51/P